CONTEÚDO DIGITAL PARA ALUNOS
Cadastre-se e transforme seus estudos em uma experiência única de aprendizado:

Entre na página de cadastro:
www.editoradobrasil.com.br/sistemas/cadastro

Além dos seus dados pessoais e dos dados de sua escola, adicione ao cadastro o código do aluno, que garantirá a exclusividade do seu ingresso à plataforma.

2856696A1072238

CB040659

Depois, acesse:
www.editoradobrasil.com.br/leb
e navegue pelos conteúdos digitais de sua coleção :D

Lembre-se de que esse código, pessoal e intransferível, é válido por um ano. Guarde-o com cuidado, pois é a única maneira de você acessar os conteúdos da plataforma.

Editora do Brasil

SÉRIE BRASIL
Ensino Médio

ENSINO MÉDIO

INGLÊS
Your Turn

1

Gisele Aga
Licenciada em Letras pelas Faculdades Metropolitanas Unidas (FMU). Autora de livros didáticos de Língua Inglesa para os anos finais do Ensino Fundamental, autora de materiais didáticos para programas bilíngues, editora de conteúdos didáticos, professora de Língua Inglesa para o Ensino Médio na rede particular de ensino e professora de Língua Inglesa em cursos de idiomas.

Adriana Saporito
Licenciada em Letras, com habilitação em Tradutor e Intérprete – Português e Inglês – pela Faculdade Ibero-Americana de Letras e Ciências Humanas. Professora de Literatura Brasileira, Língua Portuguesa e Língua Inglesa da rede particular de ensino, autora de livros de Língua Inglesa para Ensino Fundamental e Educação para Jovens e Adultos (EJA), editora de conteúdos didáticos.

Carla Maurício
Bacharel e licenciada em Letras pela Universidade Federal do Rio de Janeiro (UFRJ). Professora de Língua Inglesa da rede particular de ensino, editora de conteúdos didáticos, autora de livros de Língua Inglesa para os anos finais do Ensino Fundamental e do Ensino Médio.

2ª edição
São Paulo – 2016

COMPONENTE CURRICULAR
LÍNGUA ESTRANGEIRA MODERNA – INGLÊS
1º ANO
ENSINO MÉDIO

Editora do Brasil

© Editora do Brasil S.A., 2016
Todos os direitos reservados

Direção geral: Vicente Tortamano Avanso
Direção adjunta: Maria Lúcia Kerr Cavalcante Queiroz

Direção editorial: Cibele Mendes Curto Santos
Gerência editorial: Felipe Ramos Poletti
Supervisão editorial: Erika Caldin
Supervisão de arte, editoração e produção digital: Adelaide Carolina Cerutti
Supervisão de direitos autorais: Marilisa Bertolone Mendes
Supervisão de controle de processos editoriais: Marta Dias Portero
Supervisão de revisão: Dora Helena Feres
Consultoria de iconografia: Tempo Composto Col. de Dados Ltda.
Licenciamentos de textos: Cinthya Utiyama, Jennifer Xavier, Paula Harue Tozaki, Renata Garbellini
Coordenação de produção CPE: Leila P. Jungstedt

Concepção, desenvolvimento e produção: Triolet Editorial e Mídias Digitais
Diretora executiva: Angélica Pizzutto Pozzani
Diretor de operações: João Gameiro
Gerente editorial: Denise Pizzutto
Editor de texto: Ana Lúcia Militello, Camilo Adorno
Assistente editorial: Tatiana Pedroso
Preparação e revisão: Amanda Andrade, Carol Gama, Érika Finati, Flávia Venezio, Flávio Frasqueti, Gabriela Damico, Juliana Simões, Leandra Trindade, Mayra Terin, Patrícia Rocco, Regina Elisabete Barbosa, Sirlei Pinochia
Projeto gráfico: Triolet Editorial/Arte
Editoras de arte: Ana Onofri, Paula Belluomini
Assistentes de arte: Beatriz Landiosi (estag.), Lucas Boniceli (estag.)
Iconografia: Pamela Rosa (coord.), Clarice França
Fonografia: Maximal Estúdio
Tratamento de imagens: Fusion DG
Capa: Beatriz Marassi
Imagem de capa: Richard Paul Kane/Shutterstock.com

Dados Internacionais de Catalogação na Publicação (CIP)
(Câmara Brasileira do Livro, SP, Brasil)

Your Turn, 1 : ensino médio / Gisele Aga, Adriana Saporito, Carla Maurício. – 2. ed. – São Paulo : Editora do Brasil, 2016. – (Série Brasil : ensino médio)

Componente curricular: Língua estrangeira moderna – Inglês
ISBN 978-85-10-06463-7 (aluno)
ISBN 978-85-10-06464-4 (professor)

1. Inglês (Ensino médio) I. Saporito, Adriana.
II. Maurício, Carla. III. Título. IV. Série.

16-05817   CDD-420.7

Índice para catálogo sistemático:
1. Inglês : Ensino médio   420.7

Reprodução proibida. Art. 184 do Código Penal e Lei n. 9.610 de 19 de fevereiro de 1998.
Todos os direitos reservados

2016
Impresso no Brasil

2ª edição / 2ª impressão, 2023
Impresso na Forma Certa Gráfica Digital

Todos os esforços foram feitos no sentido de localizar e contatar os detentores dos direitos das músicas reproduzidas no CD que integra a coleção *Your Turn*. Mediante manifestação dos interessados, a Editora do Brasil terá prazer em providenciar eventuais regularizações.

Imagem de capa:
Jogo de *baseball*.

Rua Conselheiro Nébias, 887 – São Paulo/SP – CEP 01203-001
Fone: (11) 3226-0211 – Fax: (11) 3222-5583
www.editoradobrasil.com.br

Suryara Bernardi

APRESENTAÇÃO

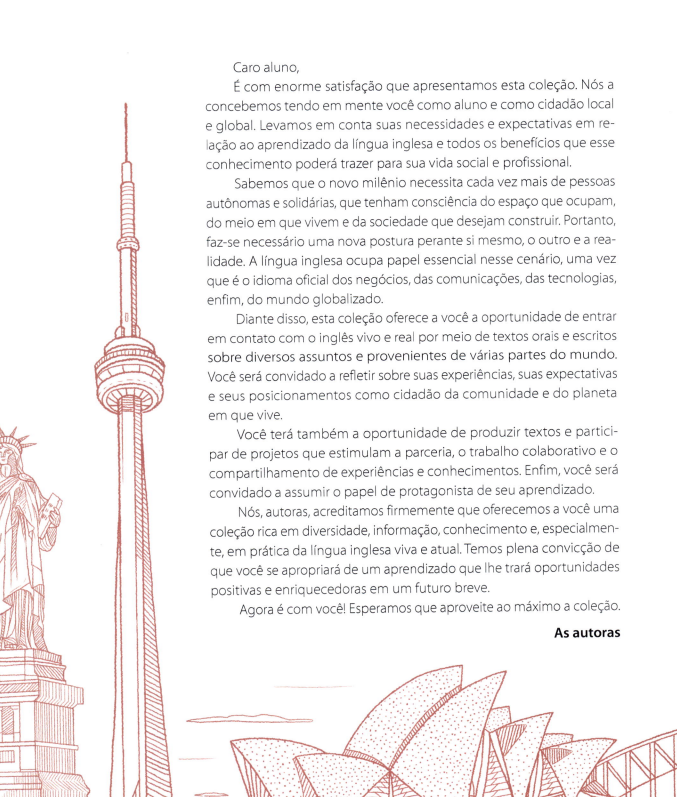

Caro aluno,

É com enorme satisfação que apresentamos esta coleção. Nós a concebemos tendo em mente você como aluno e como cidadão local e global. Levamos em conta suas necessidades e expectativas em relação ao aprendizado da língua inglesa e todos os benefícios que esse conhecimento poderá trazer para sua vida social e profissional.

Sabemos que o novo milênio necessita cada vez mais de pessoas autônomas e solidárias, que tenham consciência do espaço que ocupam, do meio em que vivem e da sociedade que desejam construir. Portanto, faz-se necessário uma nova postura perante si mesmo, o outro e a realidade. A língua inglesa ocupa papel essencial nesse cenário, uma vez que é o idioma oficial dos negócios, das comunicações, das tecnologias, enfim, do mundo globalizado.

Diante disso, esta coleção oferece a você a oportunidade de entrar em contato com o inglês vivo e real por meio de textos orais e escritos sobre diversos assuntos e provenientes de várias partes do mundo. Você será convidado a refletir sobre suas experiências, suas expectativas e seus posicionamentos como cidadão da comunidade e do planeta em que vive.

Você terá também a oportunidade de produzir textos e participar de projetos que estimulam a parceria, o trabalho colaborativo e o compartilhamento de experiências e conhecimentos. Enfim, você será convidado a assumir o papel de protagonista de seu aprendizado.

Nós, autoras, acreditamos firmemente que oferecemos a você uma coleção rica em diversidade, informação, conhecimento e, especialmente, em prática da língua inglesa viva e atual. Temos plena convicção de que você se apropriará de um aprendizado que lhe trará oportunidades positivas e enriquecedoras em um futuro breve.

Agora é com você! Esperamos que aproveite ao máximo a coleção.

As autoras

Conheça o livro

As unidades do seu livro estão organizadas por seções. Conheça um pouco mais sobre elas a seguir.

Interdisciplinaridade
Este ícone aponta as disciplinas com as quais a unidade dialoga.

Opening Pages
Seção que inicia a unidade e tem por objetivo ativar seu conhecimento prévio acerca do tema que será trabalhado, através da exploração de uma imagem. Nessas páginas você também conhecerá os objetivos da unidade.

Starting Out
Esta seção tem como principais objetivos introduzir o tema que será apresentado e aprofundado ao longo da unidade, bem como ativar seu conhecimento prévio sobre o gênero textual ao qual você será exposto.

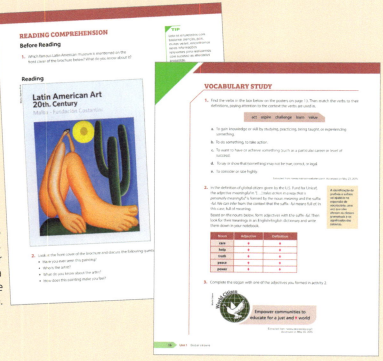

Reading Comprehension
Nesta seção, você será exposto a textos escritos de diferentes gêneros e origens, podendo desenvolver sua habilidade de leitura para compreensão geral e detalhada.

Vocabulary Study
Aqui você terá a oportunidade de estudar a língua a partir de contextos em uso presentes nos textos da seção anterior, desenvolvendo, assim, o vocabulário de maneira contextualizada.

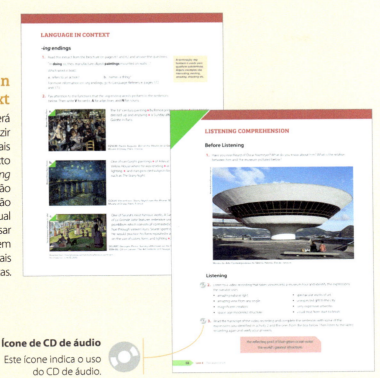

Language in Context

Nesta seção, você poderá observar a língua e deduzir as regras gramaticais a partir do texto estudado em *Reading Comprehension*. A seção termina com a subseção *Wrapping up*, na qual você é incentivado a usar as regras gramaticais em diferentes atividades orais e escritas.

Listening Comprehension

Aqui você será exposto a textos orais de diferentes gêneros e origens, podendo desenvolver sua habilidade de compreensão global e seletiva, através de variadas estratégias de audição.

Ícone de CD de áudio
Este ícone indica o uso do CD de áudio.

Speaking

Nesta seção, você participará de atividades que promovem a produção oral através da discussão de assuntos sobre o tema da unidade, usando o vocabulário e as estruturas gramaticais estudadas previamente.

Writing

Aqui você produzirá textos escritos do mesmo gênero analisado em *Reading Comprehension* e colocará em prática o vocabulário e as estruturas gramaticais estudadas na unidade, levando em consideração o propósito da produção, o público-alvo e as características do gênero.

Self-Assessment

Ao final de cada unidade, você poderá refletir e avaliar seu processo de desenvolvimento, conscientizando-se em relação aos conhecimentos adquiridos e ao que pode ser ainda aperfeiçoado.

Conheça o livro

A coleção conta ainda com os seguintes apêndices:

Further Practice
A cada duas unidades, você terá acesso a este apêndice de revisão e aprofundamento dos conteúdos apresentados nas unidades.

Exam Practice
Apêndice com questões semelhantes às das provas do Enem, também apresentado a cada duas unidades.

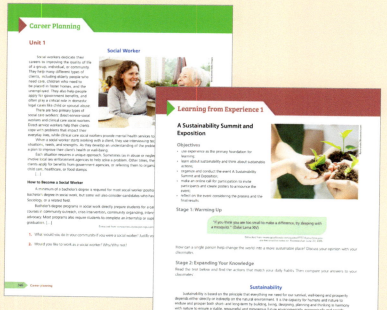

Career Planning
Aqui você poderá ler e refletir sobre algumas profissões relacionadas aos temas das unidades.

Learning from Experience
Neste apêndice, você terá a oportunidade de vivenciar experiências concretas de aprendizagem por meio de projetos interdisciplinares relacionados aos temas das unidades.

Studying for Enem

Através destas páginas, você poderá resolver as questões oficiais do Enem.

Language Reference

Apêndice de aprofundamento dos conteúdos linguísticos apresentados nas unidades, com quadros, exemplos e atividades.

Você terá acesso ainda às transcrições dos áudios, à lista de verbos irregulares e ao glossário.

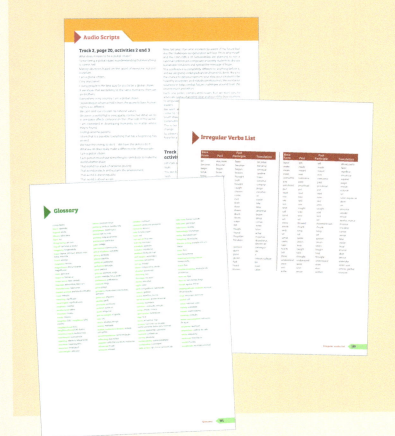

Extra Resources

Para que você possa consolidar seu aprendizado ou ainda ter acesso a novos conhecimentos além daqueles estudados em aula, recomendamos alguns artigos, vídeos, filmes etc.

Atenção!
Não escreva no livro. Todos os exercícios devem ser resolvidos no caderno.

Sumário

UNIT 1 Global Citizens 10
Starting Out 12
Reading Comprehension 13
    Global Citizen Posters 13
Vocabulary Study 16
    Suffix -ful 16
Language in Context 17
    Imperative 17
    Simple Present (Affirmative and Negative Forms:
    I, you, we, they) 18
Listening Comprehension 20
Speaking 21
Writing 22
Self-Assessment 23

UNIT 2 Take Action Now 24
Starting Out 26
Reading Comprehension 27
    Water & Sustainability in Educational Approaches 27
Vocabulary Study 30
    Suffix -al 30
Language in Context 31
    Simple Present (Affirmative and Negative
    Forms: he, she, it) 31
    Future with Will 32
Listening Comprehension 34
Speaking 35
Writing 36
Self-Assessment 37
Further Practice 1 – Units 1 & 2 38
Exam Practice 43

UNIT 3 Is Tech Killing the Music Industry? 44
Starting Out 46
Reading Comprehension 47
    Free Music Online 47
Vocabulary Study 50
    Suffix -er 50
Language in Context 51
    Adjectives 51
    Plural of Nouns 52
Listening Comprehension 54
Speaking 55
Writing 56
Self-Assessment 57

UNIT 4 The World of Art 58
Starting Out 60
Reading Comprehension 61
    Malba Flyer 61
Vocabulary Study 64
    Suffixes -ation, -sion, -tion and -ion 64
Language in Context 65
    -ing endings as Nouns, Verbs, and Adjectives ... 65
    Superlatives 66
Listening Comprehension 68
Speaking 69
Writing 70
Self-Assessment 71
Further Practice 2 – Units 3 & 4 72
Exam Practice 77

UNIT 5 Everyday Healthy Living 78
Starting Out 80
Reading Comprehension 81
    Everyday Healthy Living Quiz 81
Vocabulary Study 84
    Phrasal Verbs 84
Language in Context 85
    Simple Present: Interrogative Form and
    Wh- Question Words 85
Listening Comprehension 88
Speaking 89
Writing 90
Self-Assessment 91

UNIT 6 Sports and You 92
Starting Out 94
Reading Comprehension 95
    Beatriz Cunha's Profile 95
Vocabulary Study 98
    Cognates 98
    Collocations 98

Language in Context 99
   Simple Past 99
Listening Comprehension 102
Speaking 103
Writing 104
Self-Assessment 105
Further Practice 3 – Units 5 & 6 106
Exam Practice 111

UNIT 7 You Don't Need that Much 112

Starting Out 114
Reading Comprehension 115
   Bosch Dishwasher Ad 115
Vocabulary Study 118
   False Cognates 118
Language in Context 119
   Modal Verbs: *can*, *may* and *could* 119
Listening Comprehension 122
Speaking 123
Writing 124
Self-Assessment 125

UNIT 8 How Techy Are You? 126

Starting Out 128
Reading Comprehension 129
   A complaint e-mail 129
Vocabulary Study 132
   Phrasal Verbs 132
Language in Context 133
   Present Continuous 133
   Modal Verb: *should* 134

Listening Comprehension 136
Speaking 137
Writing 138
Self-Assessment 139
Further Practice 4 – Units 7 & 8 140
Exam Practice 145

Career Planning 146
Learning from Experience 154
Studying for Enem 162
Language Reference 166
Audio Scripts 184
Extra Resources 187
Irregular Verb List 189
Glossary 190
Bibliography 192

Suryara Bernardi

UNIT 1

GLOBAL CITIZENS

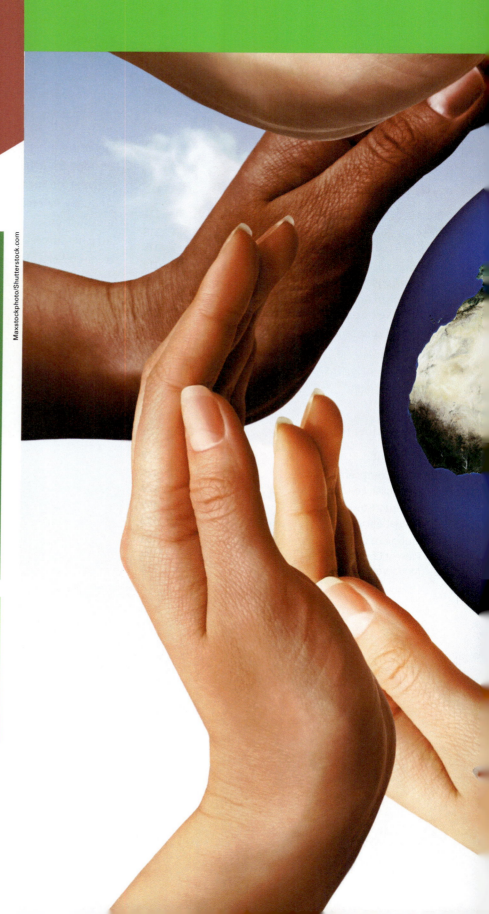

Maxstockphoto/Shutterstock.com

Nesta unidade você terá oportunidade de:

- entender o conceito de cidadania, refletir e discutir sobre contribuições pessoais para a melhoria das condições de vida no planeta;

- reconhecer os objetivos e algumas características de pôsteres e criar um;

- escutar e compreender diferentes pessoas explicando o que é ser um cidadão global;

- expressar sua opinião sobre quanto as atitudes de uma pessoa podem afetar a vida do outro.

- O que podemos ver na imagem?
- O que representam as diferentes mãos? Por quê?
- Que relação podemos estabelecer entre a imagem e o título da unidade?

STARTING OUT

1. Match the columns to find out what it means to be a global citizen. Then identify the picture which does not reflect what it means to be a global citizen.

   A global citizen is someone who…

   a. understands   • humanity everywhere

   b. challenges   • global interdependence

   c. takes action   • in a way that's personally meaningful

   d. develops   • to a better world

   e. contributes   • inequality

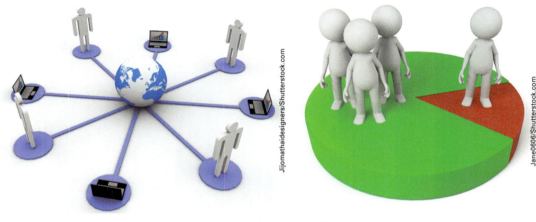

2. Based on the sentences from activity 1, write your own definition of a global citizen in your notebook. Then share your opinion with your classmates. Do you have similar ideas?

3. How much do you know about posters? Discuss these questions with a classmate.
   - What kind of information do you usually find on posters?
   - How is the information usually displayed?
   - Which visual effects are commonly used on posters?

READING COMPREHENSION

Before Reading

1. In pairs, skim the posters and discuss the following questions: What do these people have in common? Where are they from? What can you tell about their ethnicity?

Reading

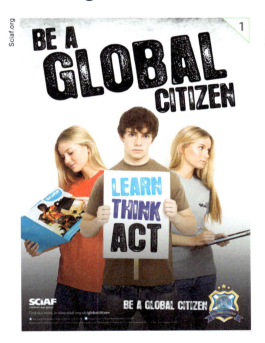
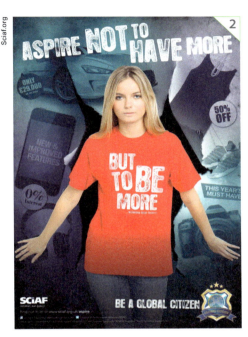

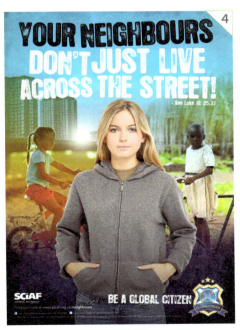

Extracted from <www.sciaf.org.uk/sciaf-schools/global-citizenship.html>. Accessed on May 30, 2015.

> **TIP**
>
> *Skimming* é uma importante estratégia de leitura que consiste basicamente em fazer uma exploração geral do texto sem se deter, a princípio, a nenhum detalhe específico. Além da leitura rápida dos parágrafos, busca-se por informações como título, datas, autor, de onde o texto foi extraído etc. Ao final dessa exploração, você saberá de que se trata o texto como um todo e, assim, sua leitura e compreensão será muito mais eficiente.
>
> Baseado em: <www.mundovestibular.com.br/articles/2588/1/TECNICAS-DE-LEITURA-DE-TEXTOS-EM-INGLES-SKIMMIMG-E-SCANNING/Paacutegina1.html>. Acessado em: 31 de outubro de 2015.

neighbours (UK)
neighbors (US)

> **TIP**
>
> Utilizar um dicionário bilíngue o ajudará a elaborar respostas significativas com mais segurança e correção, além de auxiliá-lo na aprendizagem e expansão de vocabulário da língua estrangeira. Um bom dicionário oferece muitas informações importantes, procure por elas e escreva seu texto.

2. Discuss the following questions with the whole group. After that, write down the answers.

> O Unicef (*United Nations Children's Fund*) é um fundo das Nações Unidas (ONU) e foi criado em 1946 para atender crianças em países devastados pela Segunda Guerra Mundial. Hoje a entidade atua em 190 países e territórios, incluindo o Brasil.
>
> Baseado em: <www.unicef.org/about/who/index_introduction.html>. Acessado em: 5 de fevereiro de 2015.

a. According to the U.S. Fund for Unicef a global citizen is *"someone who understands global interdependence, respects and values diversity, has the ability to challenge injustice and inequities, and takes action in a way that is personally meaningful."* Do you think the texts and images presented on the posters are in line with this definition? Do you have any suggestions to improve the posters? Justify your answers.

b. Think about the history of the community you live in. How would you change things and make it a better place to live? Explain.

c. What idea does the image behind the girl in the fourth poster convey? Justify your answer.

> **TIP**
>
> Fazer inferências significa captar o que não está dito de forma explícita no texto. São conclusões baseadas em observações. Ao fazer inferências, você estabelece relações concretas ou prováveis para concluir algo a respeito do que se captou.

3. Check the correct answers.

a. Which poster expresses the idea that people should be concerned about being better people rather than having lots of things?
- # 2
- # 4

b. What is the relation between the sentence on the boy's T-shirt and the sentence "We all have the power"?
- The sentence on the boy's T-shirt means the same as "We all have the power".
- The sentence on the boy's T-shirt is a complement of "We all have the power". When we put them together, they make sense.

c. What can you infer from poster number 4?
- We have to help people no matter where they live.
- Our next-door neighbors are the first people we have to help when they are in need.

d. Which poster presents three basic things a person has to do to be a global citizen?
- # 3
- # 1

4. The posters on page 13 are from SCIAF (*Scottish Catholic International Aid Fund*). SCIAF works to help the people in need in more than 16 countries in Africa, Asia, and Latin America. Read the posters again and choose the appropriate answers to the questions.

   a. What is the purpose of the posters?

   1. To make people change their minds and help both their local and their global neighbors.
   2. To inspire people to take action in order to help their global neighbors.

   b. What kind of language is used?

   1. The language is concise and informal.
   2. The language doesn't draw attention to the message.

   c. Where should the posters be displayed?

   1. A place where many people – especially teenagers – can see them.
   2. A place where there are many other posters.

   d. Who do the posters hope to reach? Why?

   1. They hope to reach adults.
   2. They hope to reach young people.

5. Which of the following sentences are true about posters?

   a. The target audience determines the tone of the posters.
   b. It usually takes people some time to understand the main idea.
   c. The images aren't appealing.
   d. Posters are visual communication tools.
   e. The font size is big. The background and the text are in high contrast.

6. Look at the posters on page 13 again. Write down one more characteristic that you think good posters should have.

After Reading

- If those same posters were published in Brazil, would they be effective? Why? If not, what should they be like to be effective?
- In your opinion, what's the role of education in promoting global citizenship?
- Think about the world you want for the future. Which decisions can you make now to make your view of the world real?

VOCABULARY STUDY

1. Find the verbs in the box below on the posters on page 13. Then match the verbs to their definitions, paying attention to the context the verbs are used in.

   act   aspire   challenge   learn   value

   a. To gain knowledge or skill by studying, practicing, being taught, or experiencing something.

   b. To do something, to take action.

   c. To want to have or achieve something (such as a particular career or level of success).

   d. To say or show that (something) may not be true, correct, or legal.

   e. To consider or rate highly.

   Extracted from <www.merriam-webster.com>. Accessed on May 27, 2015.

2. In the definition of global citizen given by the U.S. Fund for Unicef, the adjective *meaningful* in "[…] *takes action in a way that is personally meaningful*" is formed by the noun *meaning* and the suffix *-ful*. We can infer from the context that the suffix *-ful* means full of. In this case, full of meaning.

   Based on the nouns below, form adjectives with the suffix *-ful*. Then look for their meanings in an English-English dictionary and write them down in your notebook.

   > A identificação de prefixos e sufixos vai ajudá-lo na expansão de vocabulário, uma vez que eles alteram as classes gramaticais e os significados das palavras.

Noun	Adjective	Definition
care	♦	♦
help	♦	♦
truth	♦	♦
peace	♦	♦
power	♦	♦

3. Complete the slogan with one of the adjectives you formed in activity 2.

Empower communities to educate for a just and ♦ world

Extracted from <www.peacesites.org/>. Accessed on May 30, 2015.

Unit 1 Global Citizens

LANGUAGE IN CONTEXT

Imperative

1. Read the extracts from the posters on page 13 and choose the correct alternatives to complete the sentences.

   > **Be** a global citizen   **Learn**   **Think**   **Act**   **Aspire** not to have more but to be more

   a. The verbs in bold are in the Imperative form. They indicate
   - instructions on how to be a global citizen.
   - routine actions a global citizen performs.

   b. The idea expressed in the extract *"**Aspire** not to have more but to be more,"* is also present in…
   - *Don't aspire* to be more, but to have more.
   - *Don't aspire* to have more, but to be more.

2. Look at the Imperative forms in activity 1 again. Then match the sentences below to form rules.

   a. We use the Imperative form
   b. To form the affirmative Imperative
   c. To form the negative Imperative
   d. In the Imperative

   - we use the verb in the infinitive form without *to*.
   - we use *do not* (*don't*) before the verb.
   - to give instructions, orders, or suggestions.
   - there is no subject, but the subject *you* is implicit.

3. Read the quotes about global citizenship and complete them with the verbs from the box. Use the affirmative or negative of the Imperative forms.

   > forsake   seek   underestimate

   " ♦ the power of your vision to change the world. Whether that world is your office, your community, an industry or a global movement, you need to have a core belief that what you contribute can fundamentally change the paradigm or way of thinking about problems." (Leroy Hood, American scientist)

   Extracted from <www.brainyquote.com/quotes/quotes/l/leroyhood652766.html>. Accessed on May 30, 2015.

   "Never ♦ your motherland."
   (Lailah Gifty Akita, Ghanaian scientist)

   Extracted from <www.goodreads.com/quotes/tag/citizenship>. Accessed on October 17, 2015.

   " ♦ first to respect. Then to understand." (Jo Murphy, Australian teacher and writer)

   Extracted from <www.goodreads.com/work/quotes/25188854-global--citizens-creative-arts-text>. Accessed on May 30, 2015.

4. Unscramble the words to form basic tips on how to become a better global citizen.

a. environment / protect / the / .

b. cultures / disrespect / other / don't / .

c. any / tolerate / kind / injustice / of / don't / .

Simple Present

5. Look at these extracts from posters 3 and 4 on page 13. Then choose the correct alternatives to complete the statement.

> We all **have** the power to change the world
> Your neighbours **don't** just **live** across the street

The verb forms in bold…

a. indicate facts.
b. refer to ongoing actions.
c. are both in the affirmative form.
d. are in the Simple Present tense.

6. Pick out the correct options to complete the rules below.

a. The *Imperative / Simple Present* is used to talk about facts and generalizations, to give opinions, and to indicate habits and routines.

b. In the affirmative form of the Simple Present, we use the base form of the verb when the subject is *I, you, we,* or *they / he, she,* or *it*.

c. In the negative form of the Simple Present we use *aren't / don't* + the base form of the verb when the subject is I, you, we, or they.

Unit 1 Global Citizens

7. Complete the text using the Simple Present for facts, or the Imperative for tips. Use the verbs from the box.

> create   help   make   participate
> promote (2x)   provide   share

Global Citizen (Volunteering abroad) our programs for global citizens

♦ the world a little greener. Make a difference with our Global Citizen Environment Program.

Protecting the environment is a major part of the global development agenda. ♦ and ♦ in sustainable development projects involving pollution, climate change, conservation, waste management, and more.

Mold the minds of future leaders through our Global Citizen Education Program.

♦ provide underprivileged children and adults access to basic education. [...]

Innovate in a global setting, get to know foreign markets, start-ups, and NGOs.

Projects in this category ♦ you with hands-on experience working with NGOs and small businesses, developing relevant and culturally suitable solutions for the problems facing societies all over the world.

Develop a global mindset, ♦ your culture abroad and become a Global Citizen through our Global Citizen Cultural Understanding Program.

Projects in this category ♦ tolerance between nations and regions, and ♦ ambassadors by addressing cultural differences and origins. [...]

Extracted from <aiesecsandiego.weebly.com/volunteer-abroad.html>. Accessed on May 30, 2015.

WRAPPING UP

Imagine you are a participant in a forum about problems in your community. In pairs, think of a situation that is at the same time a local and a global concern, and write it down in your notebook. After that, come up with two suggestions to overcome the problem. Finally, share your opinion with your classmates.

LISTENING COMPREHENSION

Before Listening

1. You are going to listen to some people defining what it means to be a global citizen. Which of the following words do you expect to hear?

- access
- citizen
- difference
- humanity
- equality
- freedom
- health
- planet

Listening

2. Now listen to the recording and check if your predictions were correct.

3. Read the text and complete the sentences with the words from activity 1. Then listen to the recording again and verify your answers.

What does it mean to be a global citizen?

To me, being a global (a)♦ is understanding that everything is connected…
Making decisions based on the good of everyone, not just ourselves.
I am a global citizen.

Only one (b)♦.
Loving people is the best way for you to be a global citizen.

If we know that we belong to the same humanity then we are brothers. Everywhere is my country. I am a global citizen.

Depending on where a child is born, the (c)♦ to basic human rights is so different.
We can't limit our concern to national values.
We live in a world that is inescapably connected. What we do in one place affects someone on the other side of the world.

I am interested in developing (d)♦ no matter where they're found.
Ending extreme poverty.
I think that it is possible. Everything that has a beginning, has an end.
We have the energy to do it… We have the skills to do it.

What we do does really make a (e)♦ to other people.
I am a global citizen.
Each person must have something to contribute to make the world a better place.
That world has a lack of extreme poverty. That world protects and sustains the environment. That world is about (f)♦. That world is about access. That world is about justice. That world is about (g)♦. That world is about (h)♦.
We should have a world by now where every child is born with the same rights to life.

That's the world we are fighting for… Because the world we want and the world we're envisioning is the world we're gonna make and it's gonna be beautiful.

Transcribed from <teachunicef.org/explore/media/watch/global-citizenship>. Accessed on May 28, 2015.

Gonna é a forma reduzida de *going to*, frequentemente usada na linguagem oral.

Unit 1 Global Citizens

After Listening

Read this sentence from the recording and then discuss the questions below.

> "Depending on where a child is born, the access to basic human rights is so different."

- What are the basic human rights?
- Is access to basic human rights really different depending on where a child is born?
- In your opinion, is it possible to change this? How?

PRONUNCIATION PRACTICE

Contractions

Listen again to some sentences from the recording that contain contractions and repeat them.

We **can't** limit our concern to national values.

I am interested in developing humanity no matter where **they're** found.

And the world **we're** envisioning is the world **we're** gonna make and **it's** gonna be beautiful.

SPEAKING

In small groups, give your opinion about the following extract. Use the expressions from the box to express your views.

"What we do in one place affects someone on the other side of the world."

▶ USEFUL LANGUAGE

In my view…

From my point of view…

To my mind…

To be honest (with you)…

I'd say…

Personally, I think…

WRITING

In small groups, design posters to create awareness about global citizenship. Follow these steps.

Planning your poster

- Talk to your teacher and classmates about the concept of global citizenship and do some research about it on the Internet.
- Take notes of all the information you have collected.
- Discuss it with your group members and exchange ideas about the specific issues you want your audience to reflect on, such as overconsumption, human rights or environmental problems.
- Decide where the poster should be be displayed; for example, on your classroom wall, in the school cafeteria, in the school newspaper, or on the school website.

Writing and rewriting your text

- Plan your poster and write a draft in your notebook.
- Share the text of your poster and the images you intend to use with some groups.

> **REFLECTING AND EVALUATING**
>
> Go back to your draft and make sure you paid enough attention to the following topics:
> - ✓ Does it have an impact on the reader?
> - ✓ Do the images support the message?
> - ✓ Is the language appropriate to the target audience?
> - ✓ Can the audience quickly read the poster?
> - ✓ Is the text concise?

- Make all the necessary changes and produce your poster.

After writing

- Invite students, teachers, and school staff to view the posters and tell them everything you have learned about global citizenship. Ask them to give their opinions and exchange ideas about the issue. Have them think of the responsibility that we all share in order to build a better world.

TIP

Antes de qualquer produção escrita, pesquise o vocabulário e os elementos linguísticos que você pretende usar em sua produção. Leia e colha informações importantes sobre o assunto que deseja desenvolver. Escrever bem, tanto na língua materna quanto em língua estrangeira, requer basicamente leitura e prática.

TIP

A escrita é um processo que deve ser planejado. As etapas de revisão e reescrita são extremamente importantes, pois é por meio delas que é possível refletir sobre o texto e aprimorá-lo, não apenas no sentido de corrigir desvios gramaticais, mas também de deixá-lo mais fluente e coerente para o propósito ao qual se destina.

SELF-ASSESSMENT

Chegamos ao fim da unidade 1. Convidamos você a refletir sobre seu desempenho até aqui e responder às questões propostas abaixo, escolhendo uma das seguintes opções:

Sim.   Preciso me preparar mais.

Questões

- Com base no conceito de cidadania estudado ao longo da unidade, você é capaz de discutir sobre as contribuições pessoais que cada um de nós pode dar para a melhoria das condições de vida no planeta?
- Você se considera apto a ler e compreender diferentes pôsteres e reconhecer as características principais inerentes ao gênero?
- Você reúne conhecimentos linguístico-discursivos suficientes para produzir um pôster em inglês?
- Você se considera preparado para escutar e compreender pessoas de diferentes faixas etárias e etnias explicando o que é ser um cidadão global?
- Você se julga apto a expressar sua opinião em relação a quanto algumas atitudes de uma pessoa podem afetar a vida de outras?

Refletindo sobre suas respostas

- De que forma suas práticas de aprendizagem no decorrer desta unidade influenciaram suas respostas?
- O que você pode fazer para aprimorar ainda mais os conhecimentos adquiridos nesta unidade?
    a. Observar mais atentamente, reconhecer diferentes atitudes de cidadania expressas pelas pessoas ao meu redor e contribuir positivamente no que diz respeito às condições de vida no planeta.
    b. Ler diversos pôsteres e atentar-me para a composição de seus elementos, a fim de compreender melhor sua mensagem.
    c. Aprofundar meus conhecimentos de língua inglesa, usando recursos diversos, de forma que minha participação nas atividades seja mais ativa.
    d. Outros.

UNIT 2

TAKE ACTION NOW

Nesta unidade você terá oportunidade de:

- entender o conceito de sustentabilidade, refletir e discutir sobre sua importância para a sociedade;
- reconhecer os objetivos e algumas características de convocações e elaborar uma;
- compreender uma convocação oral para uma conferência sobre sustentabilidade;
- concordar e discordar de sugestões dadas pelos colegas sobre atitudes que podem ser tomadas para que o mundo seja mais sustentável.

- O que a imagem representa?
- Qual a intenção do artista ao reproduzir parte da obra em tons de cinza?

25

STARTING OUT  Biology Geography

1. Identify the pictures that show eco-friendly actions. Then compare your answers with a classmate.

2. Imagine that your class is organizing a workshop on sustainable water consumption and you need to invite students from other classes to make a contribution to your project. How would you encourage the other students to engage in the project? Explain your choices to your classmates.

- Handwriting notes.
- Making phone calls.
- Making posters.
- Posting an invitation or a call for participants.
- Sending text messages.
- Others.

26　Unit 2　Take Action Now

READING COMPREHENSION

Before Reading

1. Scan the text and choose the best alternative to complete the statement. The text is about...

a. political education.

b. an environmental issue.

Reading

Water & Sustainability in Educational Approaches

Training Course

13-22 March 2015 | Berlin, Germany

Call for participants from Germany, Romania, Portugal and Italy: from 13-22 March 2015 in Berlin/Germany. We expect participants who work in non-formal political education with youths/young adults or who want to do this in the future. [...]

Training workshop: Water & Sustainability in Educational Approaches from 13-22 March 2015 in Berlin/Germany. [...]

The content and activities:

Water is an essential resource for every living being. Nevertheless, the drinking water resources decreased in the last decades and the pollution of water increased while in many parts of the world water scarcity is a big problem. Effective concepts of sustainable water consumption are more important than ever. During the training we'll deal with different ecological, economic, political and social aspects of the topic water.

According to the title "Water and Sustainability in Educational Approaches" we will learn, try out and evaluate different interactive pedagogical approaches/methods, which enable us to integrate the topic water & sustainability in our future daily pedagogical work. The aim is to sensitize our learners with these attractive methods for this topic and motivate them to become active by themselves in the future. Furthermore, we'll receive background knowledge through inputs and do excursions/guided tours to different places in Berlin which are connected to water and sustainability.

> **TIP**
>
> *Scanning* é uma estratégia de leitura que consiste em uma rápida visualização do texto buscando por palavras-chaves, frases ou ideias específicas. Ao utilizarmos essa estratégia sabemos o que estamos procurando. Ao visualizar um convite, por exemplo, podemos utilizar o *scanning* para encontrar a data e o local em que ocorrerá o evento.
>
> Baseado em: <www.mundovestibular.com.br/articles/2588/1/TECNICAS-DE-LEITURA-DE-TEXTOS-EM-INGLES-SKIMMIMG-E-SCANNING/Paacutegina1.html>. Acessado em: 3 de junho de 2015.

> The Infrastructure:
>
> The training takes place in the seminar-house of the KuBiZ Cultural Center in Berlin. <www.kubiz-wallenberg.de>. Because the implementation is financially supported by the EU Program Erasmus+, the co-payment fee is only between 50-150 Euro (adapted to the individual financial capacities of the participants). The costs for the travelling, accommodation, food and the program are included in this participation fee. We'll have organic vegetarian food during the Training. The communication language will be English.
>
> If you're interested in participating, you can directly download the application form, fill it in and send it back to watertraining@tagungswerk.de.
>
> Best from Berlin, the OBUK Team.
> <tagungswerk.de/>. […]

programme (UK)
program (US)

Adapted from <www.salto-youth.net/tools/european-training-calendar/training/water-sustainability-in-educationalapproaches.4693>. Accessed on September 4, 2015.

2. The text you have just read invites…

   a. specialists to share their background knowledge about water scarcity.

   b. people from European countries to participate in a workshop about water and sustainability issues.

   c. politicians from all over the world to discuss issues related to poverty and hunger.

3. Find the incorrect information in each sentence. Then rewrite the sentences with the correct information.

   a. The participants are from North American and Asian countries.

   b. The training course is free.

   c. The communication is in different languages.

   d. The course takes place at a public library in Berlin.

4. Read "The content and activities" part of the call for participants again and answer the questions.

   a. During the training course, participants will deal with ecological, economic, political, and social aspects of the water and sustainability problem. Why are these important to discuss?

   b. Why do you think the course includes visits to water-related places in Berlin? What do you think participants can learn from those visits?

5. Choose the appropriate answers to the questions.

   a. Who is expected to attend the event?

   1. Participants who work in non-formal political education with youths/young adults or who want to do this in future.

28 Unit 2 Take Action Now

2. Anyone who is worried about the future of the planet or is a green agent in Germany, Romania, Portugal, and Italy.

b. How is the fee affordable to participants?

1. The costs for travelling, accommodation, and food are not included.

2. The event is financially supported by the Erasmus+ Program so participants can afford the fee.

c. What is the aim of the training course?

1. To help learners become active in the future, fighting for the planet and preserving water.

2. To help learners become effective green agents.

6. Read the alternatives a-f and complete the sentences below.

> a. A call for participants invites people to take part in events.
>
> b. Anyone can attend any call for participants.
>
> c. A call for participants includes different pieces of information about the event, such as date, location, and time.
>
> d. People can usually register in different formats.
>
> e. A call for participants is usually written in the third person plural.
>
> f. Participants never pay.

The true sentences about calls for participants are ♦ .

Another characteristic of calls for participants is ♦ .

After Reading

- What issues would you like to discuss or learn about in an event like the one mentioned in the text? Would the event be useful for your community? Explain.

- How can you relate the passage below extracted from the call to participants to the Brazilian context?

"Water is an essential resource for every living being. Nevertheless, the drinking water resources decreased in the last decades and the pollution of water increased while in many parts of the world water scarcity is a big problem."

VOCABULARY STUDY

1. Scan the text on pages 27 and 28 for words or phrases that have similar meanings to the ones below. After that, use two of them to complete the quotes that follow.

   a. ♦ : potable water

   b. ♦ : shortage

   c. ♦ : use

   d. ♦ : ecologically balanced

   e. ♦ : natural assets

   f. ♦ : governmental

   "Important reserves of natural ♦, like petroleum and precious metals, are the bulwarks for laying the foundations for the future." (Enrique Pena Nieto, Mexican statesman)

   Extracted from <www.brainyquote.com/quotes/quotes/e/enriquepen662940.html>. Accessed on March 27, 2016.

   "Some of the areas in China have been under very grave water ♦: for example, the north China plain; they are facing a very serious water shortage. Per capita levels have dropped to very serious levels, including in Beijing." (Ma Jun, Chinese environmentalist)

   Extracted from <www.brainyquote.com/quotes/quotes/m/majun734673.html>. Accessed on March 27, 2016.

2. Now look at the word *political* in activity 1. Does the suffix *-al* added to the noun *politics* mean *full of* or *of or relating to*?

3. Scan the text again and find other adjectives formed by the suffix *-al*, then compose and complete the chart below in your notebook. Use the definitions from the box to complete the third column.

   > of or relating to society or its organization
   >
   > of or relating to teaching
   >
   > of or relating to the ideas, customs, and social behavior of a society
   >
   > of or relating to the provision of education

Noun	Adjective	Meaning
pedagogy	♦	♦
culture	♦	♦
education	♦	♦
society	♦	♦

   Extracted from <www.oxforddictionaries.com/us>. Accessed on June 5, 2015.

LANGUAGE IN CONTEXT

Simple Present

1. Read this extract from the text on pages 27 and 28 and decide which alternatives are T (True) or F (False).

   > "The training **takes place** in the seminar-house of the KuBiZ Cultural Center in Berlin. [...]"

   The verb form in bold...

   a. expresses a routine action.
   b. doesn't indicate an opinion.
   c. indicates a command.
   d. talks about a future event.

2. Refer back to the items a-d in activity 1 and choose the correct options to complete the sentences.

   a. The Simple Present is used to talk about facts, opinions, routines, or fixed events in the *future / past*.

   b. In the Simple Present we add *-ed / -s or -es* to the verb when the subject of the sentence is the third person singular (he, she, it).

   c. In negative statements in the Simple Present, we use does not (doesn't) *after / before* the verb when the subject of the sentence is the third person singular (he, she, it).

   For spelling rules of verbs in the third person singular, go to Language Reference, page 166.

3. Use the verbs *address*, *collect*, and *invite* in the Simple Present to complete part of a call for participation.

ARL ♦ participation in the ClimateQUAL survey in 2014-2015. The online survey ♦ information about: (a) library staff perceptions of the organization's commitment to the principles of diversity, (b) staff perceptions of organizational policies and procedures, and (c) staff attitudes. The survey ♦ such issues as diversity, teamwork, learning, fairness, current managerial practices, and staff attitudes and beliefs.

[…]

Extracted from <www.arl.org/news/arl-news/3302-climatequal-organizational-climate-and-diversity-assessment-call-for-participation-2014-2015#.VXERpfnF-VN>. Accessed on June 4, 2015.

Future with Will

4. Read two other extracts from the call for participants on pages 27 and 28 and check the correct alternatives.

> "We'**ll have** organic vegetarian food during the Training."
> "The communication language **will be** English."

a. The verb forms in bold in the extracts above refer to the
- future.
- present.

b. The contracted form of *will* is
- 'd.
- 'll.

c. We use *will* for different purposes, but in the extracts above, as well as throughout the call for participants on pages 27 and 28, it indicates
- fixed future events.
- offers.
- predictions.
- spontaneous decisions.
- requests.
- promises.

For more information on Future with Will, go to Language Reference, pages 168 and 169.

5. Choose the correct options to make correct rules about the forms of will.

a. In *affirmative / negative* sentences we use will before the *auxiliary / main* verb.

b. In negative sentences we use will not or the contraction *won't / don't* before the main verb.

c. In interrogative sentences will is used *after / before* the subject. Short answers are formed with Yes + subject + will or No + subject + won't.

6. Use the prompts in parentheses to make affirmative sentences using *will*. Write them in your notebook.

Call for participants: "Speak up! Green voices in the media" seminar June 17-21

organised (UK)
organized (US)

[...]

♦ (The programme / include / practical workshops) on communicating effectively on Green issues as well as advice on managing publications with limited resources. Alongside this, ♦ (there / be / space for discussion) on the place of 'Green news' and 'Green commentary' in the public sphere in general, and how Green activists and campaigners can use these platforms to share their ideas and get their messages across. ♦ (The seminar / also address / the challenges) and potential risks or pitfalls of new digital media and how to ensure content is independent, reliable and of a high standard.

♦ (The seminar / take place / London), between Thursday the 18th and Sunday the 21st of June 2015. It is organised by the Green European Journal on behalf of GEF, with the support of the Federation of Young European Greens and Greenhouse think tank UK.[...]

Extracted from <gef.eu/event/call-for-participants-speak-up-green-voices-in-the-media-seminar>.
Accessed on June 4, 2015.

7. In your notebook, answer the questions about the invitation below.

Extracted from <africa.unwto.org/event/first-pan-african-conference-sustainable-tourism-african-national-parks>. Accessed on November 1, 2015.

a. Will the conference focus on sustainable education? If not, what will it focus on?

b. Will the event take place in Nairobi, Kenya? If not, where will it take place?

c. Will the forum take place in October?

WRAPPING UP

In pairs, look at the invitation below and take turns asking and answering questions using *will*. When you're finished, answer this question: Would you like to take part in an event like this? Explain your reasons to your classmates.

The International Green Awards for Creativity in Sustainability in association with MOSS invite you to be our guest at one of our Asia Pacific Sustainability Summits:

TOWNSVILLE Monday August 13 @ Mercure Townsville Woolcock Street
BRISBANE Tuesday August 14 @ Mercure Brisbane 85 - 87 North Quay
SYDNEY Friday August 17 @ The Menzies Sydney 144 Carrington Street
MELBOURNE Monday August 20 @ Mercure Melbourne Treasury Gardens 13 Spring Street
PERTH Thursday August 23 @ Novotel Perth Langley 221 Adelaide Terrace

"The challenges we face with climate change are not challenges at all, but incredible opportunities. In fact, I believe it to be the greatest wealth creating opportunity of our generation as we move to a post-carbon economy."

International Green Awards Judge and former Costa Rican President José-Maria Figueres

Extracted from <www.moss.org.au/Sustainability-Summit-Invitation>. Accessed on June 5, 2015.

LISTENING COMPREHENSION

Before Listening

1. Below is the logo from a conference held at the University of Western Sydney, Australia in September 2015. What do you think this conference is about?

Listening

2. Listen to Justin Whittle calling university students to participate in the conference and choose the correct alternatives.

a. Justin Whittle is
- an agriculture teacher.
- an undergraduate student.

b. One of the conference's main objectives is to empower
- people from the community to discuss sustainable solutions.
- university students to discuss sustainable solutions.

c. According to Justin, this conference is completely different because
- students will get their opinions, ideas, and solutions heard by their peers and industry professionals.
- students will pose complicated issues.

d. Justin and the UWS Office of Sustainability expect students' solutions to help combat
- future challenges surrounding food, the environment, and ethics.
- future challenges surrounding food, the environment, and health.

e. Justin invites
- university students from all over Australia.
- university students from all over the world.

> **TIP**
> Leia as perguntas antes que o professor reproduza o áudio e verifique quais são as informações de que você precisa.

3. Listen to the recording again and answer Yes or No.

a. Justin Whittle introduces himself.
b. He describes the conference.
c. Justin speaks in the first person singular.
d. The conference is directed to a particular audience.
e. The text contains hesitation pauses.

34 Unit 2 Take Action Now

After Listening

Discuss the questions below with your classmates.

- Does your school promote discussions on worldwide issues? If so, how? If not, would you like your school to promote them? Explain.
- How do school or university events like this help students become global citizens?
- Have you ever participated in an event like this? If so, what was the event about? How was it organized? If not, would you like to? Justify.

PRONUNCIATION PRACTICE

Final s sound

Listen to these verbs and pay attention to their corresponding final sound.

a. poses   /s/   /z/   **/iz/**
b. plans   **/s/**   /z/   /iz/
c. comes   /s/   **/z/**   /iz/

Now listen to the other verbs and identify the correct alternative.

d. studies   /s/   /z/   /iz/   g. reads   /s/   /z/   /iz/
e. discusses /s/   /z/   /iz/   h. plays   /s/   /z/   /iz/
f. wants   /s/   /z/   /iz/   i. gets   /s/   /z/   /iz/

SPEAKING

In small groups, discuss: Which actions can people take to help the world become more sustainable? Use the expressions from the chart to agree or disagree with your classmates' opinions.

▶ USEFUL LANGUAGE

Agreeing
I agree with you 100 percent.
I couldn't agree more.
You're absolutely right.
That's exactly how I feel.
You have a point there.

Disagreeing
I don't think so.
I'm afraid I disagree.
I totally disagree.
That's not always true.
I'm not so sure about that.

WRITING

In groups, write a call for participants to discuss issues related to the school problems or the future school events. Follow the steps.

Planning your call for participants

- Choose the topic of your call for participants. It can be about the next festivity at your school such as a *Festa Junina*, raising money or donations for charity, a sports event, collecting books for the school library, or other topics.

- Determine your target audience. The call for participants can be directed only to students, or also to teachers or all school staff.

- Ask your teacher to help decide the best date and place for the event.

Writing and rewriting your text

- Write a draft in your notebook and show it to your teacher or ask a classmate to read and make comments.

- Rewrite it, making all the necessary adjustments.

> **REFLECTING AND EVALUATING**
>
> Go back to your call for participants and make sure you paid enough attention to the following topics:
>
> ✓ Is there a catchy title?
>
> ✓ Is your audience identified?
>
> ✓ Is there an overview of the event?
>
> ✓ Is appropriate language used?
>
> ✓ Did you mention specific information such as date, time, and place?

After writing

- Discuss about the best way to publish your call for participants. It can be published on the school website or on a poster, for example.

- Be prepared to answer questions from the audience.

SELF-ASSESSMENT

Chegamos ao fim da unidade 2. Convidamos você a refletir sobre seu desempenho até aqui e responder às questões propostas abaixo, escolhendo uma das seguintes opções:

Sim.   Preciso me preparar mais.

Questões

- Você adquiriu repertório suficiente para discutir sobre a importância da sustentabilidade para a sociedade?
- Você se considera apto a ler e compreender convocações, bem como reconhecer as características principais inerentes ao gênero?
- Você reúne conhecimentos linguístico-discursivos suficientes para produzir uma convocação em língua inglesa?
- Você se sente preparado para escutar convocações e compreender a ideia principal nelas expressa?
- Você se julga apto a concordar e discordar de sugestões dadas pelos colegas sobre algumas atitudes que podem ser tomadas para que o mundo seja mais sustentável?

Refletindo sobre suas respostas

- Como você analisa a evolução do seu aprendizado em relação à unidade anterior?
- De que forma suas práticas de aprendizagem no decorrer desta unidade influenciaram suas respostas?
- O que você pode fazer para aprimorar ainda mais os conhecimentos adquiridos nesta unidade?
    a. Procurar saber mais sobre o que tem sido feito por organizações empresariais, entidades não governamentais e afins, em diferentes sociedades, em prol da sustentabilidade.
    b. Ler e escutar outras convocações e observar os elementos lexicais e linguísticos mais comumente usados.
    c. Aprofundar meus conhecimentos de língua inglesa, usando recursos diversos, de forma que minha participação nas atividades seja mais ativa.
    d. Outros.

Further Practice 1 – Units 1 & 2

1. Read the posters below. Then decide if the statements refer to the posters 1, 2, or both.

Extracted from <www.cgdev.org/blog/yes-there-such-thing-global-citizen-there-are-lots-them>. Accessed on June 3, 2015.

Extracted from <store.globalcitizen.org/collections/home-items>. Accessed on June 3, 2015.

   a. This poster is about global citizenship.

   b. The text on this poster is more concise than in the other one.

   c. It promotes an event that aims to help people in need.

   d. This poster urges people to be aware of global citizenship.

   e. This poster is visually appealing because of the contrast of colors and the size of the letters.

   f. It tells about famous artists who support the event.

   g. It shows the skyline of a big city in the background.

   h. The message is that everything we do affects people all over the world.

   i. Verbs are in the imperative form.

2. Are the posters in activity 1 addressed to the same audience? Why?

3. Use the verbs from the box to complete the text.

| ask | donate | enlist | have | join | learn | organize |
| remember | sell | share | spend | start | talk | teach |

[...]

Being a Global Citizen Means You:

1 (a) ♦ time learning about the wider world and understand the way you fit in as a global citizen. You can read newspapers, watch the news on TV, or look at news websites to find out what is going on in the world. (b) ♦ to your parents, teachers and friends about issues affecting your school, community or country, or another country. By sharing ideas, we can help come up with ways to make the world a better place.

2 (c) ♦ about and pay attention to the ways that money, politics, culture (like movies and music), technology (like the Internet), and the environment (natural resources) affect the world.

3 Learn about and respect the many different peoples and cultures in the world. (d) ♦ by getting to know the people at school and in your community and asking them about their families and backgrounds. (e) ♦ what you learn with others. (f) ♦, you can improve the world through small, everyday actions.

(g) ♦ a Game – Teach a friend or classmate a game they do not know how to play, and (h) ♦ them teach you a new game as well. This is a good way to teach others about what is special to you and to learn about other people at the same time.

Make a New Friend – (i) ♦ a classmate who doesn't usually play with your group of friends to join you in an activity. (j) ♦ a group that you don't usually play with.

International Fair – (k) ♦ an International Fair at your school. (l) ♦ students to prepare foods and/or crafts representing their cultural backgrounds. (m) ♦ tickets to family and friends and (n) ♦ the profits to an international cause, such as building classrooms in Afghanistan.

[...]

Extracted from <www.globalkidsconnect.org/global-citizen/>. Accessed on June 4, 2015.

4. The article mentions some ways to be a global citizen. In your opinion, which one is the easiest to be done? Which one is the most difficult? Why?

Further Practice 1 – Units 1 & 2

5. Look at the cartoons. Match them to the quotes that best correspond to them. There is one extra quote.

Extracted from <www.cartoonstock.com/directory/s/save_the_planet.asp>. Accessed on June 4, 2015.

Extracted from <www.cartoonstock.com/directory/c/citizenship.asp>. Accessed on June 4, 2015.

a. "I take a lot of pride in being myself. I'm comfortable with who I am." (James McAvoy, Scottish actor)

Extracted from <www.brainyquote.com/quotes/keywords/pride.html>. Accessed on June 4, 2015.

b. "We are in danger of destroying ourselves by our greed and stupidity. We cannot remain looking inwards at ourselves on a small and increasingly polluted and overcrowded planet." (Stephen Hawking, British physicist)

Extracted from <www.brainyquote.com/quotes/quotes/s/stephenhaw447569.html>. Accessed on June 4, 2015.

c. "The omission of good is no less reprehensible than the commission of evil." (Plutarch, Greek historian)

Extracted from <www.brainyquote.com/quotes/keywords/omission.html#b5r8yg6iB3phWBJo.99>. Accessed on June 4, 2015.

6. Go back to page 13 and read the poster number 2 again. It is also available in Gaelic as you can see on the poster on the right. Gaelic is a Celtic language spoken in Ireland, the Isle of Man, and the Scottish Highlands. Look at the poster on the right and answer the questions that follow.

   a. Why is the poster available in the Gaelic language?

   b. Which poster is the source, the English one or the Gaelic one? Justify your answer.

Extracted from <www.sciaf.org.uk/sciaf-schools/global-citizenship.html>. Accessed on March 27, 2016.

7. Read the call for participants and choose the best alternatives to complete it.

The student conference 2015

We are delighted to invite you to the Student Conference 2015. Here you (a) ♦ more information about the conference and registration form.

The Student Conference 2015: Education of the Future

Globalization, climate change, new technologies. The world is changing, and the university cannot stand still. Education quality (b) ♦ that we utilize the opportunities and solve the challenges that the future brings.

At the Student Conference 2015, we (c) ♦: What should education look like in the future? How can the education at the University of Oslo become as engaging and relevant to society as possible in a changing world?

The Student Parliament (d) ♦ students from all subjects and all levels to offer their opinions and take part in the discussion at the Student Conference 2015. The programme (e) ♦ of talks by invited speakers, discussions in groups and plenary debate. The conference will draft a declaration with concrete suggestions for how to increase education quality at UiO.

Attending the conference is free. We (f) ♦ all meals and accommodation from Friday to Sunday. In addition to this, you get new friends, more knowledge and a unique chance to make a difference!

Some of the topics to be discussed at the conference:

• How can the teaching be made engaging to all students?
• How should the university prepare students for the jobs and challenges of the future?
• How can digital technology be used to enhance education quality?
• What are the competencies that all university students should learn?

More information about topics and the programme will be announced. At least one of the groups (g) ♦ in English.

Published Feb 12, 2015 01:24 PM – Last modified Feb 12, 2015 01:49 PM

Extracted from <www.studentparlamentet.uio.no/english/news/2015/the-student-conference-2015.html>. Accessed on June 4, 2015.

Further Practice 1 – Units 1 & 2

    a. find / will find

    b. demand / demands

    c. ask / share

    d. invites / will invite

    e. consist / will consist

    f. cover / don't cover

    g. will work / work

8. In your notebook, write T (True) or F (False).

    a. The invitation is for a conference about education.

    b. It is directed to everyone interested in education.

    c. Extreme poverty is one of the topics of the conference.

    d. Students of all levels and subjects are welcomed.

    e. The University of Oslo wants to discuss its role in society.

9. Read the call for participants on pages 27 and 28 and identify the aspect in common between that call for participants and the one on page 41.

    a. Participants don't have to pay for anything.

    b. Both of them mention meals and accommodation to participants.

    c. English is the official language of the event.

10. The call for participants on page 41 presents four questions about some topics to be discussed at the conference. In pairs or small groups, discuss them and answer the questions taking into consideration the Brazilian context. Then share your answers with the whole class.

EXAM PRACTICE

Be a Global Citizen!

Everyone is a citizen of a country and other places on a map. There's even digital citizenship online.

Each of those types of citizenship involves membership in a group, as well as rights that are protected and responsibilities that are expected.

In school, for example, you receive an education (a right) and you must obey school rules (a responsibility).

There's a bigger community you're a part of, too, one you can be a citizen of no matter where you live. It's our planet. We're connected to people like never before, from the global economy, we're all a part of, to the air we breathe, to the technology that makes anyone's ideas just a click away. Through the United Nations, you have rights common to all people globally. You also have a responsibility to respect all people's rights and challenge global injustice. National citizenship is vital, but our common bonds and challenges are bigger than any national boarders. Embrace the world – be a global citizen!

Did you know?

The United Nations is a group of more than 190 countries that work together to promote peace and create a better world.

[...]

Extracted from <teachunicef.org/sites/default/files/documents/activities/globalcitizen_activity_9-12_8_26.pdf>
Accessed on June 4, 2015.

O texto acima é um trecho extraído de uma proposta de atividade educativa elaborada pelo Unicef (*United Nations Children's Fund*). O objetivo essencial do texto é:

a. promover o acesso à educação universal e a conscientização dos direitos educacionais das crianças.

b. promover de forma educativa a reflexão sobre a importância da cidadania global, os direitos e deveres inerentes ao seu exercício independentemente da esfera social ou geográfica em que se vive.

c. mobilizar pessoas para que sejam parceiras do Unicef e ajudem a promover os direitos das crianças e a paz no mundo.

d. promover a conscientização de que o exercício da cidadania está intimamente ligado à educação e que, portanto, a economia global e as políticas públicas devem, em conjunto, garantir o acesso a ela.

e. levantar possibilidades de exercício concreto de cidadania global e refletir sobre o quão importante é ter consciência de nossas atitudes.

UNIT 3

IS TECH KILLING THE MUSIC INDUSTRY?

Syda Productions/Shutterstock.com

Nesta unidade você terá oportunidade de:

- refletir e discutir sobre a influência da tecnologia na indústria da música;
- reconhecer os objetivos e algumas características das listas e elaborar uma;
- escutar e compreender parte de uma entrevista sobre um serviço de música digital;
- fazer uma apresentação oral sobre um serviço de música digital.

- De que maneira esta imagem representa a influência da tecnologia no cotidiano dos jovens?
- Que relação é possível estabelecer entre a imagem e o título da unidade?

Registre as respostas da unidade no caderno.

STARTING OUT

1. Complete the mind maps. Use the words *hits*, *sites*, *software*, *stations*, *online*, and *playlists*.

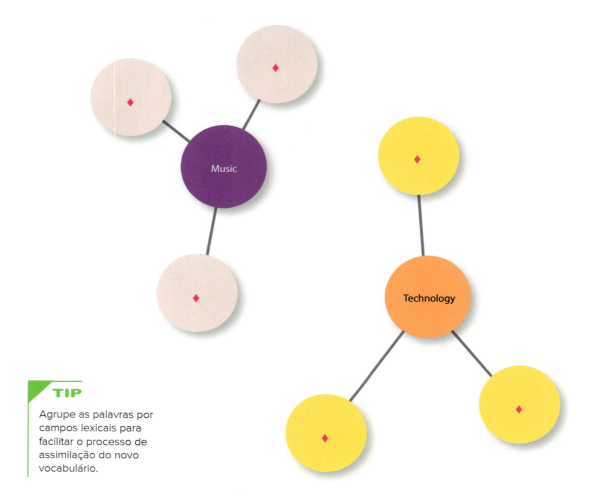

TIP

Agrupe as palavras por campos lexicais para facilitar o processo de assimilação do novo vocabulário.

2. Below you will find some statements about the influence of technology on the music industry. Identify the ones you agree with. Then discuss your answers in pairs and share your conclusions with the class.

   a. Technology makes music available to a larger number of people around the world at the touch of a button.

   b. Technology has influenced the music industry in positive and negative ways.

   c. Illegally downloading and uploading music online is considered piracy, whether for private use or not.

   d. Searching for songs and downloading them through music apps have become an integral part of most people's lives.

3. Do you know any smartphone music apps that allow us to download songs, create playlists, and access lyrics? Talk to a classmate and make a list of the music apps you can remember.

Unit 3 Is Tech Killing the Music Industry?

READING COMPREHENSION

Before Reading

1. Scan the text and discuss the answers to these questions with a classmate: What are the listed items about? Would you be interested in reading about them? Why/Why not?

Reading

Free Music Online
The Best Sites for Free Online Radio and Music Downloads
By Erin Huffstetler
Frugal Living Expert

Looking for free music that you can listen to online or download to your MP3 player? Here are several great sites to check out, starting with the best:

1. Rdio
Enjoy free music at home and on the go. Rdio gives you access to over 20 million songs, and allows you to customize your listening experience. Stream full-length albums and stations or create your own playlists.

2. Spotify
Listen to your favorite songs, albums, stations and playlists for free. Just download the software, and start listening. The "Discover" tab makes music recommendations based on your listening habits.

3. Pandora.com
Enter a favorite artist, song or composer; and the site will create a custom radio station featuring your favorite music, plus other music like it. You can create up to 100 radio stations, and tweak the playlists until they're just right.

4. Jango.com
Jango is online radio gone social. Enter an artist's name, and it'll play songs by that artist, along with songs recommended by other users who like the same artist. You can create your own custom playlists, view other people's playlists and chat with other music fans about your favs.

5. NPR.com
Download songs, studio sessions and concerts. There's also a different, full-length album to listen to each week and a Song of the Day newsletter.

6. Live Music Archive
Listen to free recordings of live concerts from thousands of bands across all genres.

7. Amazon.com
Choose from over 46,000 songs that are available for free download. It may not be the latest hits, but the price is right.

Want to save more money? Sign up for the Frugal Living newsletter, and get a fresh batch of tips delivered to your inbox each week.

Extracted from <frugalliving.about.com/od/frugalfun/tp/Free_Music_Online.htm>. Accessed on June 24, 2015.

2. Refer to the list of online music sources on page 47 and decide if the statements below are true or false.
   a. At Pandora.com users can create a dozen radio stations.
   b. Rdio allows users to access millions of songs.
   c. The "Discover" tab from Spotify makes random music recommendations to users.
   d. At Live Music Archive you can listen to live concerts for free.

3. Read the list on page 47 again. Consider the items from 1 to 7 and number the statements below accordingly.
   a. It is not the best, but it has good prices.
   b. You have to download the software before listening to music.
   c. Users can listen to live concerts.
   d. It allows chatting with the users.
   e. It offers a newsletter.
   f. Users can stream full-length albums and stations.
   g. It can adapt playlists to fit users' preferences.

4. Norwegians under 30 were asked by the international Federation of the Phonographic Industry whether they illegally download music online. Look at the pie charts below and discuss these questions with a classmate: Why do you think the number of people admitting illegally downloading files has decreased so much? Do you think this has happened in Brazil as well?

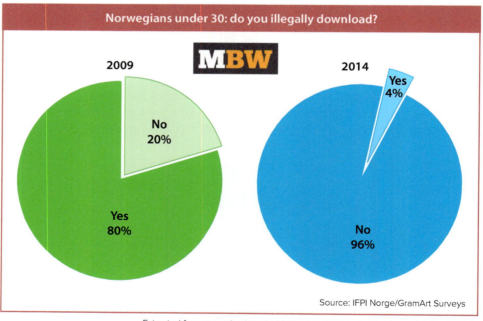

Source: IFPI Norge/GramArt Surveys

Extracted from <www.businessinsider.com.au/norway-music-piracy-statistics-2015-1>. Accessed on November 5, 2015.

Unit 3 Is Tech Killing the Music Industry?

5. Read the lists below and compare them to the one on page 47. Then choose the true sentences about their characteristics.

Bath & Body
- ✓ Hand lotion
- ✓ Chapstick
- ✓ Deodorant
- ✓ Contact solution (when I wore them)
- ✓ Toothbrush and mini-toothpaste
- ✓ Bath wipes to help you freshen up
- ✓ Face wipes or mini bottle of face wash and wash cloth

Extracted from <herpackinglist.com/2012/02/carry-on-packing-essentials>. Accessed on November 5, 2015.

Kitchen
- ✓ Wipe down countertops and cabinets (start at immediate right of the stove).
- ✓ Clean face of appliances (refrigerator, microwave, dishwasher).
- ✓ Wipe down stove top.
- ✓ Clean inside the microwave.
- ✓ Soak stove drip pans and knobs in sink.
- ✓ Clean inside and around sink.
- ✓ Sweep and mop floor (go light on cleaning product in the water to avoid build-up).

Adapted from <www.mollymaid.com/cleaning-institute/schedules-charts-checklists/house-cleaning-checklist.aspx>. Accessed on November 5, 2015.

a. Lists are a series of items put together and related to the same issue.
b. They can present some explanation about the items.
c. They present instructions.
d. Discourse markers are always used.
e. The items can be indicated by numbers or bullet points.
f. Lists are usually used when the author wants to organize information.

6. Mention some examples of lists present in your everyday life. Then share with your classmates.

After Reading

- In your opinion, which site mentioned on page 47 is the most useful? Why?
- When you download music or videos, do you worry about the legality of what you're doing? Justify your answer.
- Does everybody have access to streaming services in your community? If so, what's the most popular service among them? If not, why?

Is Tech Killing the Music Industry? **Unit 3**

VOCABULARY STUDY

1. Match the verbs from the list on page 47 to their corresponding meanings in context.

> customize   download   feature   stream   tweak

a. ♦: transmit or receive (data, especially video and audio material) over the Internet as a steady, continuous flow.

b. ♦: modify (something) to suit a particular individual or task.

c. ♦: have as a prominent attribute or aspect.

d. ♦: copy (data) from one computer system to another, typically over the Internet.

e. ♦: *informal* improve (a mechanism or system) by making fine adjustments to it.

Extracted from <www.oxforddictionaries.com/us>. Accessed on June 24, 2015.

TIP

Tente montar um glossário e criar frases significativas com os novos vocábulos. Essas estratégias facilitarão seu aprendizado.

2. The suffix -er was added to the verb *play* to form the noun *player* in "Looking for free music that you can listen to online or download to your MP3 **player**?"
What does this suffix indicate?

a. It indicates what or who performs an action.

b. It indicates an action in progress.

3. Compose the chart below in your notebook and then complete it accordingly. The first one is done for you.

Verb	Noun	Meaning
teach	teacher	person who teaches
print	♦	machine that prints
act	♦	♦
direct	♦	♦
speak	♦	♦
photograph	♦	♦
refrigerate	♦	♦

4. Choose 2 nouns from activity 3 and write meaningful sentences using them in your notebook.

LANGUAGE IN CONTEXT

Adjectives

1. Choose the correct alternatives to complete the sentences about this extract from the list on page 47.

   "Looking for **free** music that you can listen to online or download to your MP3 player? Here are several **great** sites to check out, starting with the best:"

   a. The words *free* and *great* ♦.
   - describe an action or a state
   - qualify nouns

   b. *Free* qualifies ♦. *Great* qualifies ♦.
   - music / MP3 player
   - music / sites

   c. *Free* and *great* are ♦.
   - adjectives
   - nouns

2. Read another extract from the list on page 47 and find the adjectives that qualify the noun *album*.

   > "Download songs, studio sessions and concerts. There's also a different, full-length album to listen to each week and a Song of the Day newsletter."

3. Now compare the structures below and complete the sentences.

English		Portuguese	
free	music	música	gratuita
↓	↓	↓	↓
adjective	noun	noun	adjective

   > Lembre-se de que os adjetivos também podem ser posicionados após o verbo *to be*: *Music is free.*

   a. In English and in Portuguese, adjectives are used to add more information to ♦, qualifying or describing them.

   b. In ♦, adjectives often come before nouns and do not have plural forms.

   c. In ♦, adjectives often come after nouns and have plural forms.

4. Match adjectives and nouns from the chart to complete the first two items of the *Top Library Apps for 2015* list, on the following page.

Adjectives	Nouns
adventurous	artists
favorite	music
free	music service
legendary	user

Is Tech Killing the Music Industry? Unit 3 — 51

Top Library Apps for 2015

[...]
Here is our list of five apps you won't know how you lived without.

#1 – Freegal Music

Download and listen to your ♦ for free with Freegal, a ♦ from Livingston Parish Library. All you need is your library card number.

Freegal offers access to about 7 million songs, including Sony Music's catalog of ♦. The collection is comprised of music from over 28,000 labels with music that originates in more than 80 countries.
[...]

#2 – LS2 Mobile

[...]
With LS2 Mobile, you can search our catalog, reserve or renew books, check your account, and more. For the ♦, the app even randomly selects books from our suggested reading lists.
[...]

Extracted from <www.mylpl.info/top-library-apps-2015>.
Accessed on June 8, 2015.

catalogue (UK)
catalog (US)

Plural of Nouns

5. Read another extract from the text on page 47 and identify the words that are in the plural. Then read the statements, choose T (True) or F (False), and correct the false ones in your notebook.

> "Listen to your favorite songs, albums, stations and playlists for free. Just download the software, and start listening. The 'Discover' tab makes music recommendations based on your listening habits."

Em inglês, para formarmos o plural regular, também é possível acrescentar -*es* aos substantivos, dependendo de sua terminação: o instrumento musical *bass* (baixo), por exemplo, é acrescido de -*es* na forma plural.

a. The plural words identified above are adjectives.

b. The letter -*s* was added to those nouns to form their plurals.

For irregular plurals and spelling rules of regular plurals, go to Language Reference, page 171.

6. Complete the text on the folowing page with the plural form of the nouns from the box.

> company   economy   expert   number
> platform   process   ringtone   vendor

52   Unit 3   Is Tech Killing the Music Industry?

How Big Is Africa's Music Industry?
Ringtone Sales In Nigeria: $150M

By Dana Sanchez
Published: August 8, 2014, 5:23 pm

Nigerian popstar D'Banj, aka Africa's Bono, said this week on ABCTV that the music industry is Africa's biggest export after oil and gas.

Not true, according to TampaBayTimes' PolitiFact.

[…]

Industry (a) ♦ and academics say it's hard to calculate just how much the music industry is worth in Africa, PolitiFact reports.

That's because there's piracy, no one's keeping track formally, and the distribution system is street (b) ♦ who may reprint content after paying a one-time fee, according to Aidbee Adiboye, a spokesperson for Chocolate City Group, one of Africa's largest entertainment (c) ♦.

"The protection of intellectual property throughout the region remains a concerning issue," said Jenny Mbaye, who studies African cultural production at the University of Cape Town. "In this sense, the piracy challenge calls for actively confronting and redressing the persisting lack of information and poor documentation of the (d) ♦ that animate the chain of production and labor dynamics in these (e) ♦."

Informal statistics from Nigerian entertainment executives show that (f) ♦ sold to the tune of $150 million in 2011, global live performances brought in an additional $105 million, and album sales reached $30 million in 2008 (three times more than 2005), PolitiFact reports.

Nollywood, Nigeria's film industry, is the second largest in the world after Bollywood according to the U.N., bringing in $250 million in annual revenue, according to the Financial Times.

These (g) ♦ represent total revenue, not export revenue and they provide a general idea of how the industry is doing.

And the African music industry is doing really well, especially in D'Banj's home country of Nigeria as it moves to digital (h) ♦.

[…]

Extracted from <afkinsider.com/68131/big-africas-music-export-industry>. Accessed on November 4, 2015.

WRAPPING UP

Choose one of the seven sites for free online radio and music downloads listed on page 47 and write a short description about it. Remember to follow the word order of adjective + noun. Read your description to your classmates and listen to their descriptions as well.

LISTENING COMPREHENSION

Before Listening

1. Look at the logos below. What do they refer to?

    a. Apps for downloading free music.

    b. Music streaming services.

Listening

2. Jimmy Kimmel is an American comedian and writer who is the host and producer of "Jimmy Kimmel Live", ABC Television Network's late-night talk show. Listen to part of his interview with the American rapper Jay Z and answer: What are they talking about?

3. Listen again and choose the correct answers to these specific questions.

    a. What's the name of the music streaming service?
        • Spotify   • Tidal
    b. Who is the owner of the service?
        • Jay-Z   • Calvin Harris

c. According to Jay Z, how does this service compare to other services?
- He says it is better due to the sound quality.
- He says the sound is better, but that's only a part of why his service is better.

d. Why are different artists interested in this service?
- Because its owner is also an artist.
- Because they want to go in the same direction the music is going.

After Listening

Discuss the following questions with your classmates.
- Have you ever heard of Tidal? If so, what had you known about it before you listened to Jay Z? If not, would you be interested in trying to use it? Why/Why not?
- Do you use a music streaming service? Which one? What did you consider when choosing it? If you haven't signed up for one, would you like to? How would you choose one?
- What are the benefits of signing up for a streaming service? Justify.

SPEAKING

Present a music streaming service to your classmates. Follow these steps.

✓ Choose any music streaming service.
✓ Research it on the Internet.
✓ Take notes in your notebook.
✓ Prepare what you are going to say in your presentation. Use full sentences.
✓ You can use dictionaries to help with the vocabulary needed or you can ask your teacher for help.
✓ Discuss your presentation with your teacher. Take into consideration the comments he/she makes and improve what you are going to say, if necessary.
✓ Rehearse your presentation.
✓ Present your music streaming service to the class. Speak as naturally as you can.
✓ Be prepared to answer your classmates' questions.

WRITING

Write a list of the technological devices you use in your everyday life. Follow the steps below.

Planning your list

- Think about different aspects of your daily routine and how technological devices are used to make them easier and better.
- Select the devices you use the most, for example: smartphone, notebook, digital camera, e-book reader, portable media player, tablet etc.

Writing and rewriting your text

- Write a draft of your list in your notebook. Include a small paragraph to explain why each device makes your life easier and better.
- If necessary, refer back to activity 5 on page 49.

> **REFLECTING AND EVALUATING**
>
> Go back to your list and make sure you paid enough attention to the following topics:
> - ✓ Did you organize it using bullet points or numbers?
> - ✓ Is the language appropriate for its purpose?
> - ✓ Can readers find information quickly?
> - ✓ Are grammar and punctuation correct?

- Show your list to the teacher.
- Make all the necessary changes after your teacher's correction.

After writing

- Share your list with your classmates and compare the similarities and differences the kinds of technology listed.
- Are there more similarities or differences among students in your class?

SELF-ASSESSMENT

Chegamos ao fim da unidade 3. Convidamos você a refletir sobre seu desempenho até aqui e responder às questões propostas abaixo, escolhendo uma das seguintes opções:

Sim.

Preciso me preparar mais.

Questões

- Você tem conhecimento suficiente para expor sua opinião acerca da influência da tecnologia no cotidiano dos jovens, bem como na indústria da música?
- Você se sente capaz de ler e compreender diferentes listas em língua inglesa e reconhecer as características principais inerentes ao gênero?
- Você reúne conhecimentos linguístico-discursivos suficientes para elaborar uma lista em língua inglesa?
- Você está preparado para escutar entrevistas sobre os serviços de música digital e compreender informações específicas?
- Você se julga apto a fazer uma apresentação oral sobre um serviço de música digital?

Refletindo sobre suas respostas

- Como você analisa a evolução do seu aprendizado em relação à unidade anterior?
- De que forma suas práticas de aprendizagem no decorrer desta unidade influenciaram suas respostas?
- O que você pode fazer para aprimorar ainda mais os conhecimentos adquiridos nesta unidade?
    - **a.** Buscar por mais informações sobre a influência da tecnologia no cotidiano das pessoas, em especial dos jovens, bem como na indústria da música.
    - **b.** Ler diferentes listas e identificar elementos lexicais e estruturais inerentes ao gênero.
    - **c.** Aprofundar meus conhecimentos de língua inglesa, usando recursos diversos, de forma que minha participação nas atividades seja mais ativa.
    - **d.** Outros.

UNIT 4

THE WORLD OF ART

Nesta unidade você terá oportunidade de:

- refletir e discutir sobre o papel do museu e instituições similares como espaços de educação não formal;
- reconhecer os objetivos e algumas características de folhetos e criar um;
- escutar e compreender o áudio de um *tour* em vídeo em um museu brasileiro;
- pesquisar sobre um museu brasileiro de arte e fazer uma apresentação oral usando *slides*.

- Que forma de manifestação artística podemos reconhecer na imagem?
- A qual movimento em especial essa forma de manifestação artística está diretamente ligada?
- Este mural foi pintado por um artista brasileiro. Você consegue identificá-lo? Justifique.

Man sitting in front of a mural painted by graffiti artist Eduardo Kobra in Parque Ibirapuera, São Paulo, Brazil, 2015.

STARTING OUT Art History

1. Match these famous pieces of art to the information about them below.

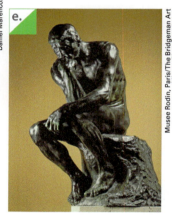
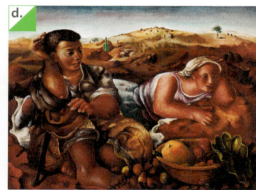

- DI CAVALCANTI, Emiliano. *Ciganos*, 1940. Oil on canvas, 97 × 130 cm. Museu Nacional de Belas Artes, Rio de Janeiro, Brazil.
- DA VINCI, Leonardo. *Mona Lisa* (*La Joconde*), c. 1503-6. Oil on panel, 77 × 53 cm. Louvre Museum, Paris, France.
- RODIN, Auguste. *The Thinker*, 1881. Bronze Sculpture, 71,5 × 40 × 58 cm. Rodin Museum, Paris France.
- MUECK, Ron. *Couple Under An Umbrella*, 2013. Sculpture, 300 × 400 × 500 cm.
- SANTANA, Leo. *Carlos Drummond de Andrade*, 2012. Bronze Sculpture life size, 150 kg. Copacabana beach, Rio de Janeiro, Brazil.

2. In pairs, answer the questions below. Then report your answers to the class.

   a. How do you find out about art events in your neighborhood?

   b. Are brochures from museums and art galleries good ways for people to get information about art exhibitions? Do you ever read any? Why/Why not?

READING COMPREHENSION

Before Reading

1. Which famous Latin American museum is mentioned on the front cover of the brochure below? What do you know about it?

> **TIP**
> Leia os enunciados com bastante atenção, pois, muitas vezes, encontramos neles informações relevantes para realizarmos com sucesso as atividades propostas.

Reading

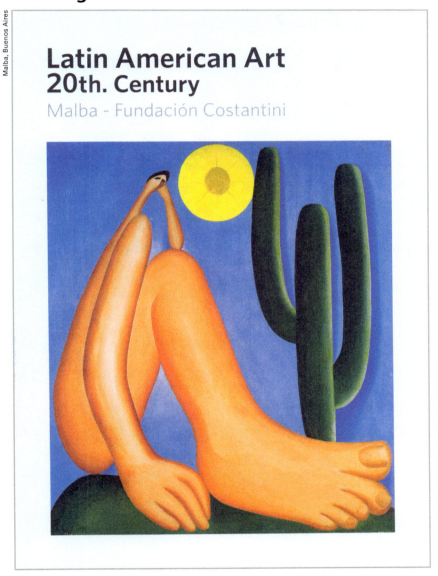

Malba, Buenos Aires

2. Look at the front cover of the brochure and discuss the following questions in small groups.
- Have you ever seen this painting?
- Who is the artist?
- What do you know about the artist?
- How does this painting make you feel?

3. Read the inside page of the brochure and check the sentences you can infer.

> # Latin American Art 20th. Century
> ## Malba - Fundación Costantini
>
> Abstract and non-figurative tendencies are part of the international history of art since the beginnings of the 20th century. Wanting to deviate from the illusionist origins of painting and from the concept of the painting as a "window to the world", they use different alternatives to free the visual arts from their initial objective of representing reality. In the mid-forties, Buenos Aires turned into one of the most active centers of Concrete Art and its variations. Madí, Asociación Arte Concreto Invención and Perceptísmo are the three groups formed by Argentines such as Gyula Kosice and Enio Iommi, and Uruguayans such as Rhod Rothfuss and Carmelo Arden Quin, to contribute to the international debate of Concretism. The artists use material elements of visual language, such as forms, colors, lines, and planes. Their works replace the traditional octagonal framework with irregular and unevenly- cut contours and investigate the function of layers of color and of the system of structures in series. They also invent articulated and transformable "sculptures" and resort to industrial materials such as lacquers, glass and bakelite. In doing so, they manufacture object-paintings mounted on walls and aerial mobiles hanging in space. In the decade of the 50s, Alejandro Otero paints his series of white abstractions with chromatic lines in Caracas, while Brazilians Hélio Oiticica and Lygia Clark turn color and light into bodies that materialize as the spectator observes them. In the same decade and the following, Julio Le Parc and Abraham Palatnik construct boxes and artifacts that investigate the physical and perceptive experience of sight, adding to it the concept of real or illusory movement and the active participation of the viewer, both possibilities opened by optic and kinetic art.

Malba, Buenos Aires

a. Abstract and non-figurative tendencies have a degree of independence from visual references in the world.

b. Hélio Oiticica's and Lygia Clark's works of art interact with the spectator.

c. Latin American artists had no say in the debate on Concretism.

d. The works of art described in the text depict a natural object or scene.

e. Brazilian artists prefer using cool colors.

4. Look at two of Tarsila do Amaral's paintings and answer the questions.

DO AMARAL, Tarsila. *O Lago*, 1928. Oil on canvas, 75,5 × 93 cm. Private Collection Hecilda and Sergio Fadel, Rio de Janeiro, Brazil.

DO AMARAL, Tarsila. *Caipirinha*, 1923. Oil on Canvas, 60 × 81 cm. Collection Salim Taufic Schahin, São Paulo, Brazil.

   a. In your opinion, which one belongs to the same period as Abaporu, that is, the Anthropophagic Movement? Explain.

   b. What do you know about this artistic movement?

5. Look for one characteristic of brochures that is NOT true.

Brochures…
- have a title on the front cover, an interesting layout, and appealing images.
- are usually found in museums, institutions, and places tourists visit.
- include relevant information.
- are often kept and referred to again and again.
- are usually distributed to people that are interested in learning more about something.
- are only printed on one side.

6. Add another true characteristic about brochures.

After Reading

- Have you ever been to a museum? If so, share your experience. If not, what kind of museum would you like to visit? Why?
- Do you think that museums are important in education? Justify your answer.
- Do you admire any Brazilian artists? If so, who and why? If not, would you like to learn more about Brazilian artists? Explain.

The World of Art **Unit 4**

VOCABULARY STUDY

1. Refer to the text on page 62 to infer the meaning of the words in bold below, and then choose their correct synonyms.

   a. "Wanting to **deviate** from the illusionist origins of painting…"

   - keep
   - differ

   b. "… Alejandro Otero paints his series of white abstractions with **chromatic** lines in Caracas, …"

   - colorful
   - pale

   c. "… both possibilities opened by optic and **kinetic** art."

   - static
   - dynamic

   TIP
   Procure sempre observar o contexto em que as palavras são usadas para inferir seu significado corretamente.

2. Read the definitions of two art terms, pay attention to the underlined words, and choose the correct word to complete the sentence.

   Installation
   A form of art, developed in the late 1950s, which involves the <u>creation</u> of an enveloping aesthetic or sensory experience in a particular environment, often inviting active engagement or <u>immersion</u> by the spectator.

   Wet-<u>collodion</u>
   A photographic process invented in 1848 by F. Scott Archer, in which a glass plate, coated with light-sensitive <u>collodion emulsion</u>, is placed in a camera, exposed, developed, and varnished for <u>protection</u> before being used to create prints.

   Extracted from <www.moma.org/learn/moma_learning/glossary>. Accessed on June 13, 2015.

   The suffixes *-ation*, *-sion*, *-tion*, and *-ion* form *nouns / verbs*. They indicate names of actions, processes, states, conditions, or results.

3. Complete the chart with nouns which have suffixes from activity 2. Then choose the correct meaning.

Verb	Noun	Meaning
admit	♦	• entrance restriction • entrance permission
collect	♦	• accumulation • addition
direct	♦	• communication • instruction
exhibit	♦	• representation • exposition

LANGUAGE IN CONTEXT

-ing endings

1. Read this extract from the brochure on pages 61 and 62 and answer the questions in your notebook.

"In **doing** so, they manufacture object-**paintings** mounted on walls…"

Which word in bold...

a. refers to an action? **b.** names a thing?

For more information on *-ing* endings, go to Language Reference, page 172.

> A terminação *-ing* também é usada para qualificar substantivos. Alguns exemplos são *interesting*, *exciting*, *amazing*, *shocking* etc.

2. Pay attention to the functions that the *-ing* ending words perform in the sentences below. Then write V for Verbs, A for Adjectives, and N for Nouns.

The 19th century painting ♦ by Renoir portrays working ♦ class people dressed up and enjoying ♦ a Sunday afternoon at the Moulin de la Galette in Paris.

RENOIR, Pierre Auguste. *Ball at the Moulin de la Galette*, 1876. Oil on canvas, 131 x 175 cm, Musée d'Orsay, Paris, France.

One of van Gogh's paintings ♦ of Arles at a riverbank not far from the Yellow House where he was residing ♦ at the time. The night scenery, lighting ♦, and stars provided subjects for his more famous paintings, such as *The Starry Night*.

GOGH, Vincent van. *Starry Night over the Rhone*, 1888. Oil on canvas, 72.5 x 92 cm, Musée d'Orsay, Paris, France.

One of Seurat's most famous works, *A Sunday Afternoon on the Island of La Grande Jatte* features extensive use of a technique known as pointillism, which consists of contrasted color dots that form a single hue through viewers' eyes. Seurat spent over two years on this piece. He would practice his form repeatedly at the park, concentrating ♦ on the use of colors, form, and lighting ♦.

SEURAT, Georges Pierre. *Sunday Afternoon on the Island of La Grande Jatte*, 1884-86. Oil on canvas, 207.5 x 308.1 cm. The Art Institute of Chicago, IL, USA.

Adapted from <totallyhistory.com/art-history/famous-paintings>. Accessed on June 13, 2015.

3. Use the -ing form of the words from the box to complete the invitation below.

feature   open   paint   park   view

Extracted from <www.graffitisouthafrica.com/news/categories/exhibition>. Accessed on June 13, 2015.

Superlatives

4. Read another extract from the brochure on pages 61 and 62 and choose the correct alternatives to complete the sentences.

"In the mid-forties, Buenos Aires turned into one of **the most active** centers of Concrete Art and its variations."

a. In this extract, Buenos Aires is compared to…

- the mid-forties.
- all the centers of Concrete Art in the world.

b. To compare one object or person in a group of three or more things or people we use the…

- superlative forms of adjectives.
- comparative forms of adjectives.

Unit 4   The World of Art

5. Choose the correct options to complete the rules for the superlative forms of adjectives in English.

> **Irregular Superlatives**
> **bad** = the worst
> **good** = the best

  a. We often use the article *a / the* before adjectives in the superlative form. In some cases, other determiners such as possessives, for example, are used.

  b. To form the superlative of long adjectives, we use *more / the most* before them, whereas *-est* is added to short adjectives.

6. The extracts below are interpretations of famous paintings. Complete them with the superlative form of the adjectives in parentheses.

  a. Limbourg Brothers (Pol, Herman, Jean) (fl.1390-1416)

  Tres Riches Heures du Duc de Berry (1413)

  Gouache on vellum, Musee Conde, Chantilly

  One of ♦ (magnificent) examples of Medieval miniature painting, this illuminated manuscript is the showpiece of the Musee Conde, in Chantilly.

  Extracted from <www.visual-arts-cork.com/famous-paintings/#limbourg>. Accessed on June 13, 2015.

  b. Eyck, Jan Van (1390-1441)

  [...]

  Arnolfini Portrait (1434)

  Oil on wood, National Gallery, London

  Painted in Bruges and crammed with complex symbolism, this work is one of ♦ (famous) panel paintings of the 15th century Flemish School of painting.

  Extracted from <www.visual-arts-cork.com/famous-paintings/#eyck>. Accessed on June 13, 2015.

  c. Weyden, Roger Van der (c.1400-1464)

  Descent From the Cross (Deposition) (c.1435-40)

  Oil on panel, Prado, Madrid

  This masterpiece of Flemish religious art is Van der Weyden's ♦ (great) work, and one of ♦ (influential) works of the mid-15th century.

  Extracted from <www.visual-arts-cork.com/famous-paintings/#weyden>. Accessed on June 13, 2015.

  d. Vermeer, Jan (1632-1675)

  [...]

  The Lacemaker (c.1669-1670)

  Oil on canvas, Louvre, Paris

  Vermeer's ♦ (small) picture, it is regarded as one of ♦ (great) genre paintings created during the period of Dutch Realism.

  Extracted from <www.visual-arts-cork.com/famous-paintings/#vermeer>. Accessed on June 13, 2015.

WRAPPING UP

In pairs, take turns answering the questions below. Then report your answers to your classmates and listen to theirs as well. Do you share the same opinions?

From your point of view:
What's the most interesting form of art?
Which is the best museum in your city?
Who are the most famous Brazilian painters and sculptors?
How can new artists promote their work?

LISTENING COMPREHENSION

Before Listening

1. Have you ever heard of Oscar Niemeyer? What do you know about him? What is the relation between him and the museum pictured below?

Museu de Arte Contemporânea de Niterói, Niterói, Rio de Janeiro, 2013.

Listening

2. Listen to a video recording that takes viewers into a museum tour and identify the expressions the narrator uses.

- amazing natural light
- amazing view from any angle
- magnificent creation
- space-age modernist structure

- spectacular works of art
- unexpected gift to the city
- very expensive artworks
- visual treat from start to finish

3. Read the transcript of the video recording and complete the sentences with some of the expressions you identified in activity 2 and the ones from the box below. Then listen to the video recording again and verify your answers.

> the reflecting pool of blue-green ocean water
> the world's greatest attractions

68   Unit 4   The World of Art

"Hi! I'm Naomi, and I'm very excited to show you ♦.

This ♦, designed by Oscar Niemeyer, houses the Niterói Contemporary Art Museum.

Situated at the bottom of a cliff, with a spectacular beach and view of surrounding small islands and distant mountains, this museum provides visitors with more than spectacular works of art.

♦ beneath the structure was intended by Niemeyer to be the likeness of a flower.

The wall of windows surrounding the entirety of the building provides amazing natural light as well as an ♦.

Finished in 1996, it has quickly become one of Brazil's national treasures.

From the intricate spiraling walkway to the view from the courtyard and beautiful art housed inside, this museum is a ♦.

Thank you for watching our Travel Video series.

See you next time!"

Transcribed from <www.youtube.com/watch?v=WQnxUpuS13U>. Accessed on June 14, 2015.

After Listening

Discuss these questions with your classmates.

- In your opinion, does Naomi show excitement when she talks about the museum? Justify your answer.
- Do you feel like watching the video? Why?
- Now that you have listened to the recording, are you interested in visiting the museum? Explain.

PRONUNCIATION PRACTICE

The [ŋ] sound

Listen to these words and pay attention to the sound [ŋ].

    amazing   reflecting   surrounding

Now listen to the words below and identify the ones that are pronounced with [ŋ].

bring	building	dance
lunch	mountain	museum
sing	spiraling	watching

SPEAKING

In pairs, prepare a picture-based slide presentation about any other Brazilian museum.

✓ Choose a museum and research it in magazines, books, or on the Internet.

✓ Look for pictures of the building, its location, and any other features that would be interesting to show your classmates. Do not choose more than four pictures.

✓ Show the pictures to your teacher. Tell him/her what you plan to talk about with each picture.

✓ Present your slides to your classmates.

✓ Be prepared to answer your classmates' questions.

WRITING

In pairs, follow the steps below to create your own brochure.

Planning your brochure

- Exchange ideas with your classmate about a place in your community you would like to learn more about such as a public library, a museum or a park.
- Do some research about the place on the Internet.
- Take notes about aspects of the place that make your choice special or interesting.
- Think about the images you can use to create an attractive layout.

Writing and rewriting your text

- Write a draft of your text in your notebook and show it to your teacher.
- Ask a classmate to read your text and give his/her opinion about it.

> **REFLECTING AND EVALUATING**
>
> Go back to your brochure and make sure you paid attention to the following topics.
> - ✓ Does it have attractive images?
> - ✓ Is the language appropriate to your target audience?
> - ✓ Does it contain relevant and interesting information?
> - ✓ Did you plan it so that both sides are printed on?

- Make all the necessary adjustments, insert the images, and produce the final version of your brochure on an A4 sheet of paper.

After writing

- Make some copies and distribute them among your classmates.

SELF-ASSESSMENT

Chegamos ao fim da unidade 4. Convidamos você a refletir sobre seu desempenho até aqui e responder às questões propostas abaixo, escolhendo uma das seguintes opções:

Sim.   Preciso me preparar mais.

Questões

- Você é capaz de identificar diferentes formas de manifestação artística, bem como reconhecer a qual movimento elas estão ligadas?
- Você reúne argumentos suficientes para discutir sobre o papel do museu e de instituições similares como espaços de educação não formal?
- Você está apto a ler e compreender diferentes folhetos e reconhecer as características principais inerentes ao gênero?
- Você reúne conhecimentos linguístico-discursivos para criar um folheto em inglês?
- Você está preparado para escutar e compreender áudios de *tours* em vídeo em museus?

Refletindo sobre suas respostas

- Como você analisa a evolução do seu aprendizado em relação à unidade anterior?
- De que forma suas práticas de aprendizagem no decorrer desta unidade influenciaram suas respostas?
- O que você pode fazer para aprimorar ainda mais os conhecimentos adquiridos nesta unidade?
    a. Buscar por mais informações sobre diferentes formas de manifestação artística, os movimentos aos quais elas estão diretamente ligadas e o que eles expressam.
    b. Ler diferentes folhetos de museus em língua inglesa, para ampliar meu vocabulário e identificar as estruturas linguísticas comumente usadas nesse gênero textual.
    c. Aprofundar meus conhecimentos em língua inglesa, usando recursos diversos, de forma que minha participação nas atividades seja mais ativa.
    d. Outros.

Further Practice 2 – Units 3 & 4

1. Complete the following article using the adjectives from the box. Then identify the nouns they refer to.

> accessible   casual   extensive   fresh   legitimate   unsurprising

Music piracy in Australia drops 20%
By Nicola Riches | 10 September 2014

Online music piracy has declined a staggering 20% in Australia during the past year, according to ♦ data published by Spotify, which claims its streaming services are playing a part in the reduction.

Unveiled at the government's Copyright – Online Infringement public forum in Sydney last night, Spotify's director of economics, Will Page, explained that the ♦ streaming site has gone some way to help reduce file-sharing in the region over the past two years.

A statement from Spotify explained that ♦ file-sharers (of music) are dropping off, even though the hard-core base remains relatively unchanged.

Page also revealed a perhaps more ♦ statistic that TV/film piracy in Australia, during the same 12 months, was four times higher than piracy traffic generated by music files – a period which didn't even include the US airing of Game of Thrones.

Page says, "It's exciting to see that we are making in-roads into reducing the music piracy problem within such a short space of time in this market. It shows the scope for superior legal services [offered at an ♦ price point] to help improve the climate for copyright online.

"Let's be clear, Australia still faces a massive challenge in turning around its much talked about media piracy challenge, and it always has, and always will, take a combination of public policy and superior legal offerings", he adds.

Working with analytics company MusicMetric, Spotify completed an ♦ study of piracy on Bit Torrent sites in Australia. The full findings from the report will be unveiled at a music industry conference in Brisbane today.

Choice is currently making noise over the relative high prices it says Australians pay for digital TV content and running a campaign attacking the Government's efforts to stem illegal dowloading.

Extracted from <www.adnews.com.au/news/music-piracy-in-australia-drops-20>.
Accessed on November 6, 2015.

2. Pick out the only statement that is not true according to the text.

a. Spotify states that its services help to reduce music piracy online.

b. The combination of public policy and superior legal offerings has solved the problem of piracy in Australia.

c. According to Will Page, Australians still illegally download movies.

3. Refer to the pie chart on page 48 and answer: What do Norway and Australia have in common when it comes to illegal music downloads?

4. In your notebook, draw a pie chart to illustrate the decline of music piracy in Australia.

5. Read the cartoon and decide whether the statements below are true or false.

Extracted from <www.glasbergen.com/cartoons-about-music>. Accessed on June 24, 2015.

   a. The men are in a hospital.

   b. They seem to be friends.

   c. A pacemaker is a small device used to control heart rhythms.

   d. Pandora is a music streaming service.

   e. The patient got the first pacemaker.

6. The cartoon conveys an unlikely future of streaming services. How do you think these services will be offered in 10 years? Explain.

Further Practice 2 – Units 3 & 4

7. Scan the brochure below and answer: Have you ever heard of D'Orsay Museum? Where is it located?

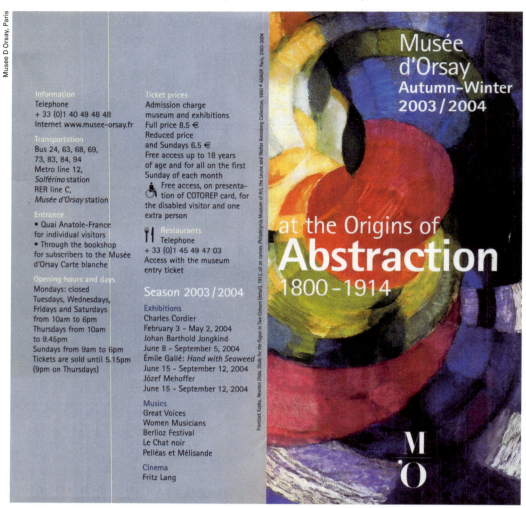

The Museum and its collection

The museum is housed in the former Gare d'Orsay, a train station designed by Victor Laloux, built from 1898 to 1900. The collections — painting, sculpture, architecture, but also graphic and decorative art, photography and music — cover the period ranging from 1848 to 1914, a still-recent era marked by historical, political and social upheavals, by the development of a diversity of literary and artistic movements, including realism and impressionism, and by the emergence of modernity, which explains the fascination it exercises on visitors.

Visits in English

Masterpieces of the Musée d'Orsay
From November to February :
From Tuesday to Saturday at 11.30am,
except November 1 and 11, December 25
and January 1

The Impressionists
November and January :
Tuesdays at 2.30pm except November 11
All year : Thursdays at 4pm
except December 25 and January 1

From Van Gogh to Matisse
December and February :
Tuesdays at 2.30pm

Duration 1h30 / Information + 33 (0)1 40 49 48 48
Full price 6 € / Reduced price 4,5 €

8. Compare the brochure above to the one on page 61. In pairs, discuss their similarities. Then share your findings with the whole class.

9. Find the best options to complete the text below. If necessary, use a dictionary to help you understand the words you don't know.

> ### The Art of Seeing Art™
>
> The average person spends 17 seconds (1) *looking / understanding* at a work of art in a museum. It usually takes much less time than that to identify an image. But (2) *looking / understanding* it? That requires (3) *slowing down / looking at* and taking the time to see the details. This kind of thoughtful, (4) *general-looking / close-looking* helps us to see that things are not always as they appear at first glance.
>
> The Art of Seeing Art™ is a process for looking carefully and (5) *exploring / seeing* a work of art on a deeper level. Developed by the Toledo Museum of Art, The Art of Seeing Art™ is a series of six steps – Look, Observe, See, Describe, Analyze, and Interpret – that you can use when looking at any work of art in the Museum's collection or any image in everyday life.
>
> [...]

Extracted from <www.vislit.org/the-art-of-seeing-art>. Accessed on June 24, 2015.

10. What can we infer about the text above?

I. Looking at a work of art requires enough time so that you can feel it and understand it.

II. It is unlikely that we can immediately understand a work of art and all its meaning.

III. Most people can observe and make an in-depth analysis in a few seconds.

IV. The Toledo Museum of Art developed a helpful way to guide visitors so they can have a deeper understanding of the art pieces.

a. I, II and III.

b. Only IV.

c. I, II and IV.

d. Only II.

e. All of them.

11. What do you think you should look for when looking at a work of art?

Further Practice 2 – Units 3 & 4

12. Look at the poster and answer the questions.

The exhibition will be available in selected cinemas. Do you think this kind of initiative makes art more accessible to people? Why/Why not?

Extracted from <www.themoviehouse.net/index.php/site/special_events/fathom_events_exhibition_2015>. Accessed on June 26, 2015.

13. The three works of art presented on the poster are called *The Railway*, *The Scream*, and *A Young Woman standing at a Virginal*, respectively. Read the extracts below and write the name of the paintings they refer to.

   a. […] The richly dressed lady playing a virginal stands in a prosperous Dutch home with paintings on the wall, a marble-tiled floor, and a skirting of locally produced Delft blue and white tiles. The two paintings on the wall behind her cannot be identified with certainty.

   Extracted from <www.nationalgallery.org.uk/paintings/johannes-vermeer-a-young-woman-standing-at-a-virginal>. Accessed on April 29, 2016.

   b. […] Its androgynous, skull-shaped head, elongated hands, wide eyes, flaring nostrils and ovoid mouth have been ingrained in our collective cultural consciousness.

   Extracted from <www.khanacademy.org/humanities/becoming-modern/symbolism/a/munch-the-scream>. Accessed on April 29, 2016.

   c. […] With her back to us, a young girl stands looking through a fence. Facing us directly, a woman sits with a small dog in her lap and a book in her hand. Billowing steam from an unseen train obscures the center background, but the edge of a bridge juts out at right, identifying the setting as Gare Saint-Lazare—Paris' busiest train station and emblem of the city's unsettling 19th-century makeover.

   Extracted from </www.nga.gov/content/ngaweb/Collection/highlights/highlight43624.html>. Accessed on April 29, 2016.

EXAM PRACTICE

Observe o quadro *Guernica* (1937) do pintor espanhol Pablo Picasso e leia o texto que o acompanha.

Guernica shows the cataclysms of war as well as the anguish and destruction it inflicts upon people, especially innocent civilians. This painting has attained an enormous reputation over the years, and has become an everlasting reminder of the devastation of war, in addition to becoming an anti-war icon. [...]

Extracted from <totallyhistory.com/guernica>. Accessed on September 3, 2015.

PICASSO, Pablo. *Guernica*, 1937. Oil on canvas, 349 × 776 cm. Museo Nacional Centro de Arte Reina Sofia, Madrid, Spain.

As pinturas abaixo também são de Pablo Picasso e foram produzidas em diferentes datas. Em quais delas você pode perceber o mesmo tema universalista observado em Guernica?

I.

PICASSO, Pablo. *Massacre in Korea*, 1951. Oil on canvas, 110 × 210 cm. Musée Picasso, Paris, France.

III.

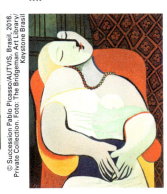

PICASSO, Pablo. *Le Rêve* (*The Dream*), 1932. Oil on canvas, 130 × 97 cm. Private Collection of Steven A. Cohen.

II.

PICASSO, Pablo. *The Weeping Woman*, 1937. Oil on canvas, 60 × 49 cm. National Gallery of Victoria, Melbourne.

IV.

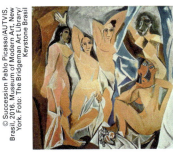

PICASSO, Pablo. *Les Demoiselles D'Avignon*. (*The Young Ladies of Avignon*), 1907. Oil on canvas, 243.9 × 233.7 cm. Museum of Modern Art, New York, U.S.

a. Nas obras I e II podemos observar o universalismo cujo foco é vocação social e humanista.
b. Apenas a obra I retrata o mesmo sofrimento visto em *Guernica*.
c. Nenhuma das obras retrata temas universais.
d. As obras II e III mostram características universais como *Guernica*, pois a discriminação da mulher ocorre em qualquer lugar e situação.
e. Na obra IV há o mesmo universalismo de *Guernica*, pois denuncia a exploração e o sofrimento das mulheres.

UNIT 5

EVERYDAY HEALTHY LIVING

MaraZe/Shutterstock.com

Nesta unidade você terá oportunidade de:

- refletir e discutir sobre hábitos de uma vida saudável;
- reconhecer os objetivos e algumas características de *quizzes* e elaborar um;
- escutar e compreender o áudio de um vídeo de uma nutricionista sobre alimentos saudáveis para o café da manhã;
- participar de uma interação oral sobre seus hábitos alimentares.

- O que podemos ver na imagem?
- Que relação podemos estabelecer entre a imagem e qualidade de vida?
- Por que esta imagem apresenta um apelo estético tão forte?

STARTING OUT

 Biology
Physical Education

1. What does healthy living mean to you? Match the pictures to the actions below. Then identify the ones that represent healthy living to you.

- eating healthy food
- exercising frequently
- having fruit as a snack

- meditating
- spending quality time with friends
- drinking water

2. Read the statements below and decide whether they are healthy dieting Myths (M) or Facts (F).

   a. Eating late at night makes you gain weight.
   b. The fewer meals you have, the better.
   c. Being overweight and physically inactive can cause diabetes.
   d. Not all carbohydrates are bad for your health.
   e. Your stomach will shrink if you eat less.
   f. Breakfast is the most important meal of the day.

3. Quizzes are very popular, whether published on websites, in magazines, or in newspapers. What kind of quiz do you usually take? Do you like to take health quizzes? Justify your answer.

READING COMPREHENSION

Before Reading

1. Scan the text and answer: What text genre is it? What is its objective?

> **TIP**
> Ao ler um texto, procure reconhecer nele características que o ajudem a descobrir a qual gênero textual ele pertence. Essa estratégia pode lhe ajudar na compreensão geral, uma vez que textos do mesmo gênero tendem a ser organizados e estruturados de modo similar.

Reading

<healthfinder.gov/Quiz/Question/everyday-healthy-living-quiz/10-24_11-27>

1 How often do you eat fast food?

- [ ] Every day
- [ ] Every week
- [ ] Once a month
- [ ] Almost never

Submit ▶

How often do you eat fast food?

- [ ] Every week

Fast food can be tempting. But did you know that fast food is almost always high in calories, fat, sugar and, sodium (salt)? Try to find restaurants that offer healthier choices, like salads and fruits.

> **Tip**
> Next time you order a pizza, ask for less cheese to cut down on sodium and fat.

Next ▶

Change Answer

2 How do you manage stress?

- [ ] I like to plan ahead and decide which tasks I need to do first.
- [ ] I take time to relax (like by breathing deeply, walking or meditating).
- [ ] I get active.
- [ ] Other

Submit ▶

How do you manage stress?

- [ ] I get active.

Getting active is a great way to manage stress!

> **Tip**
> Planning your tasks ahead of time can also help manage stress. Try writing a to-do list to help you figure out what's most important and how to manage your time. You can even schedule in time to exercise!

Next ▶

Change Answer

3 How well do you usually sleep?

- ▨ Great. I sleep through the whole night.
- ▨ Not very well. I have trouble falling asleep.
- ▨ It depends. My sleep changes a lot.

Submit ▶

How well do you usually sleep?

- ▨ Not very well. I have trouble falling asleep.

Try setting a bedtime routine:

Go to bed at the same time every night.

Aim for 7 to 8 hours of sleep each night.

Make sure your bedroom is dark and quiet.

Avoid eating, talking on the phone, or watching TV in bed.

> **Tip**
> If you are still awake after staying in bed for more than 20 min, get up.
> Do something relaxing (like reading a book in another room) until you feel sleepy.

Change Answer

Adapted from <healthfinder.gov/Quiz/Question/everyday-healthy-living-quiz/10-24_11-27#>.
Accessed on June 15, 2015.

2. In your notebook, write T (True), F (False), or NM (Not Mentioned).

   a. The person who took the quiz doesn't like fast food.

   b. If you cut down on some fatty ingredients, your meal will be healthier.

   c. The person who took the quiz leads a sedentary life.

   d. Being physically active can make people even more stressed.

   e. Most people organize their lives doing the most important things first.

   f. Lack of sleep can affect your longevity.

3. Read the tip about stress again and work in pairs to write two more tips that can help people manage stress. Then report them to the class.

4. The quiz on page 81 is about healthy living. The questions and answers you have read are related to eating habits, stress, and sleep. What other issues do you think should be mentioned in a quiz about healthy living? Justify your answer. Then share your view with the class.

5. Read the passage below which contains some tips to healthy eating. Then work in pairs to add more items to the list about things that are important to limit.

> […]
> To eat healthy, be sure to get plenty of:
> - Vegetables, fruits, whole grains, and fat-free or low-fat dairy products
> - Seafood, lean meats and poultry, eggs, beans, peas, seeds, and nuts
>   It's also important to limit:
> - Sodium (salt)
> - Added sugars – like refined (regular) sugar, brown sugar, corn syrup, high-fructose corn syrup, and honey
>   […]

Extracted from <healthfinder.gov/HealthTopics/Category/everyday-healthy-living/nutrition/eat-healthy>. Accessed on March 29, 2016.

6. Read the sentences about quizzes and identify the true ones.

   a. The title of the quiz usually indicates its topic.

   b. Quizzes only contain two or three questions.

   c. Quizzes can be published in newspapers or magazines, or on websites.

   d. They usually present more than one possible answer for each question.

   e. They can be organized in multiple-choice, true-or-false, yes-or-no, or mixed questions.

   f. The questions in quizzes are usually simple and direct.

7. Look for the only characteristic that is NOT true about quizzes.

   a. The questions usually have three or four possible answers.

   b. Some quizzes have some sort of feedback that supports the correct answers.

   c. They invite people to take part in events.

   d. Question words are used to create multiple-choice questions.

   e. Quizzes have results that analyze the respondents' answers.

After Reading

- How would you answer the questions in the quiz on pages 81 and 82? Which tips do you think you would get?
- Do you have a healthy lifestyle? If so, explain. If not, how could you change your lifestyle to make it healthier?
- In your opinion, what is the first step to start living a healthy life? Explain.

VOCABULARY STUDY

1. Unscramble the letters to form words extracted from the quiz on pages 81 and 82. Then use these words to complete the excerpts below. Write in your notebook.

   a. s/f/o/d/o

   b. u/a/g/r/s

   c. r/c/l/s/i/o/e/a

   d. a/t/f

   […] Different ♦ can be used by the body to produce different amounts of energy. Carbohydrate e.g. ♦ contains less than 4 calories, whilst fat contains 9 calories per gram. This means 5 g sugar in a product has about 20 calories, whilst 5 g fat has 45 calories. Therefore a good way to decrease the ♦ in your food is to lower the amounts of ♦. But just because a food is labelled fat-free, it doesn't mean it is calorie-free. Indeed, most fat-free foods still provide a lot of calories from carbohydrates and proteins. […]

   Extracted from <www.eufic.org/page/en/page/FAQ/faqid/weight-gain-fat-calories-sugar/>. Accessed on June 15, 2015.

   e. d/u/s/m/i/o

   f. t/s/l/a

   […] High consumption of ♦, one of the components in table ♦, is a well-established risk factor for high blood pressure and cardiovascular diseases. Reducing intakes to recommended levels would benefit public health and therefore efforts to achieve this are being made by national authorities, non-governmental organisations and food industry. […]

   organisations (UK)
   organizations (US)

   Extracted from <www.eufic.org/article/en/nutrition/salt/artid/addressing-salt-intakes-in-Europe/>. Accessed on June 15, 2015.

2. Refer to the quiz on pages 81 and 82. In the sentences, "Next time you order a pizza, ask for less cheese to **cut down** on sodium and fat." and "Try writing a to-do list to help you **figure out** what's most important and how to manage your time", the phrasal verbs **cut down** and **figure out** mean...

   - reduce and understand
   - increase and understand
   - reduce and start

3. The phrasal verbs below are related to healthy living and dieting. Match them to their definitions and write them down in your notebook. If necessary, refer to the Glossary on pages 190 and 191 for help.

   bolt down   put on   work out

   a. to ♦: to eat food very quickly

   b. to ♦: to do physical exercise as a way of keeping fit

   c. to ♦ (weight): to become fatter

   Extracted from <www.macmillandictionary.com/>. Accessed on June 14, 2015.

LANGUAGE IN CONTEXT

Simple Present: Interrogative Form and *Wh-* Question Words

1. Read the questions from the quiz on pages 81 and 82 and match the two parts below to form meaningful sentences.

   "**How often do** you eat fast food?"

   "**How do** you manage stress?"

   "**How well do** you usually sleep?"

   a. To form interrogative sentences in the Simple Present, we use ♦

   b. *Wh-* questions begin with a question word (What, When, Where, Who, How etc.) ♦

   c. We use *How often* ♦

   d. We use *How* ♦

   e. *How well* is used ♦

   - followed by the auxiliary verb, the subject, and the main verb in the base form.

   - to ask about the degree of quality.

   - *do* when the subjects are I, you, we, or they, and *does* when the subjects are he, she, or it.

   - to ask in what manner or by what means.

   - to ask about frequency.

   For more *Wh-* Question Words, go to Language Reference, pages 174 and 175.

2. Use the *wh-* question words from the box to complete a few questions adapted from the quiz entitled *How healthy are you*? Then answer them in your notebook.

   > How many   How much   How often

   a. ♦ servings of fruit do you usually eat in a day, including fresh, canned, and dried fruit?

   b. ♦ moderate (breathing quicker than normal) or vigorous (huffing and puffing) exercise do you usually do in a day?

   c. ♦ do you spend time doing active things with your family (like playing at home, walking the dog, cycling, or swimming)?

   Adapted from <www.healthykids.nsw.gov.au/kids-teens/kids-activities/healthy-kids-quiz.aspx>.
   Accessed on March 15, 2016.

3. Use the prompts from the boxes to complete the comic strips' questions in the Simple Present.

that / count   you / watch

a.

Extracted from <www.thecomicstrips.com/store/add.php?iid=58594>. Accessed on June 15, 2015.

how / you / figure that   it / ever stick around

b.

Extracted from <www.thecomicstrips.com/store/add.php?iid=41164>. Accessed on June 15, 2015.

4. Unscramble the words to form questions about living a healthy lifestyle. Then take turns with a classmate to answer them orally with true information about yourself.

   a. lifestyle / you / a / Do / healthy / have / ?

   b. a / Does / role / your / stress / life / play / big / in / ?

   c. eating / What / you / does / mean / healthy / to / ?

   d. do / How many / night / sleep / every / hours / you / ?

5. Read two excerpts from the text *Rise and Shine – What kids around the world eat for breakfast*. Then, in your notebook, write questions for the answers provided.

> [...]
> **Emily Kathumba, 7 years old, Chitedze, Malawi**
> Emily lives with her grandmother Ethel on the outskirts of Lilongwe, Malawi's capital. Because Ethel works in another family's home – doing cleaning, cooking and child care – her extended family of nine rises before 6 a.m. to eat breakfast together before they disperse to work and school. [...] When she can, Emily likes to drink sweet black tea in the mornings, a common beverage for Malawian children.

Extracted from <www.nytimes.com/interactive/2014/10/08/magazine/eaters-all-over.html?_r=1>. Accessed on June 15, 2015.

a. ♦
Answer: They live on the outskirts of Lilongwe, Malawi's capital.

b. ♦
Answer: When she can, Emily likes to drink sweet black tea in the mornings.

> **Aricia Domenica Ferreira, 4 years old, and Hakim Jorge Ferreira Gomes, 2 years old, São Paulo, Brazil**
> Aricia's pink sippy cup is full of chocolate milk, but her brother Hakim's cup contains coffee (*café com leite*). For many Brazilian parents, coffee for kids is a cultural tradition; the taste evokes their own earliest memories. Many also believe that coffee provides vitamins and antioxidants and that a small milky serving in the morning helps their children concentrate in school. [...]

Extracted from <www.nytimes.com/interactive/2014/10/08/magazine/eaters-all-over.html?_r=1>. Accessed on June 15, 2015.

c. ♦
Answer: Aricia's sippy cup contains chocolate milk.

d. ♦
Answer: For them, the taste of coffee evokes their own earliest memories.

e. ♦
Answer: Many parents believe that coffee provides vitamins and antioxidants.

WRAPPING UP

In your notebook, write three questions about eating habits that you would like to ask your classmate. You can ask, for example: What do you have for breakfast? How often do you have family meals? Take notes and then write the answers to his/her questions. Finally, compare your answers. Do you have similar habits?

LISTENING COMPREHENSION

Before Listening

1. You are going to listen to the nutrition coach Lisa Neilsen talk about the healthiest breakfast foods. In your notebook, write the items you think she suggests her clients have.

milk

oatmeal

omelet

berries

papaya

peanut butter

eggs

whole grain cereal
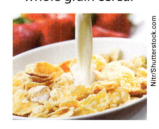

fruit salad

yogurt

fruit smoothies

whole grain toast

Listening

 2. Now listen to Lisa and check if your predictions were correct.

 3. Listen to Lisa again and write T (True) or F (False). Then correct the false statements in your notebook.

  a. Lisa says she's always surprised when she finds out how many of her clients don't start their day off with a healthy breakfast.

  b. In her view, when we skip breakfast we put unnecessary strain on the body.

  c. Lisa says people should have a huge and sweet sugary breakfast.

  d. She usually has whole grain bread with peanut butter for breakfast, no matter what kind of day she is going to have.

  e. She helps her clients balance out their meals in a way they fuel their bodies for the most active times of the day.

After Listening

What can you infer from the extract below? Share your ideas in small groups. Then listen to the other groups' views and discuss.

> "We can have lunch for breakfast, we can have dinner for breakfast, we can have any food that we think is gonna fuel us for the kind of day we are gonna be having."

PRONUNCIATION PRACTICE

The /e/ sound

Listen and pay attention to the sound of the letter in bold.

b**e**rries /e/

Now listen to these words and find the ones that have the same sound.

br**e**ad	br**e**akfast	c**e**real
ch**ee**se	**e**ggs	p**e**anut

SPEAKING

Imagine you're going to a nutrition coach because you want to change your eating habits. What kind of questions do you think he/she will ask you? Exchange your ideas with a classmate.

Exchange ideas with the whole group. Did you come up with the same questions? How different are your answers from your classmates'? What can you infer from this comparison?

WRITING

In pairs, follow the steps below and create a quiz to challenge your classmates.

Planning your quiz

- Talk to your classmate and choose a topic to focus on. You can create a quiz about sports, movies, arts, literature, festivities and celebrations, eating habits, historical events, or another topic that interests you.
- Do some research and decide how many questions you are going to write.
- Decide who the target audience is and where the quiz will be published.
- Choose a meaningful and catchy title.
- Think about the number of questions and decide on their structure: multiple-choice, true or false questions, or a mix of styles.
- Talk to your classmate and define what the quiz results will be.

Writing and rewriting your text

- Write a draft of the quiz in your notebook.

> **REFLECTING AND EVALUATING**
>
> Go back to your quiz and make sure you paid enough attention to the following topics:
> - ✓ Is the title meaningful and catchy?
> - ✓ Are the questions direct and challenging?
> - ✓ Are there three or more response options?
> - ✓ Does it have results that analyze the answers?

- Don't forget to write an answer key with the correct answers.
- Exchange quizzes with another pair of students and discuss them.
- Make all the necessary adjustments and write your quiz out on a sheet of paper.
- Make some copies and distribute them to your target audience.
- If possible, publish your quiz online on the school website.

After writing

- Present an overview of the results to your class.
- Vote for the most interesting and creative quiz.

SELF-ASSESSMENT

Chegamos ao fim da unidade 5. Convidamos você a refletir sobre seu desempenho até aqui e responder às questões propostas abaixo, escolhendo uma das seguintes opções:

Sim.   Preciso me preparar mais.

Questões

- Você é capaz de identificar hábitos de vida saudável e discutir sobre sua importância no cotidiano das pessoas?
- Você se considera apto a responder a *quizzes* de assuntos pessoais?
- Você reúne conhecimentos linguístico-discursivos suficientes para produzir um *quizz* em inglês?
- Você se considera preparado para escutar áudios de vídeos de nutricionistas e compreender as dicas sobre os alimentos que devem ser consumidos nas diferentes refeições do dia?
- Você se julga apto a participar de uma interação oral sobre seus hábitos alimentares?

Refletindo sobre suas respostas

- Como você analisa a evolução do seu aprendizado em relação à unidade anterior?
- De que forma suas práticas de aprendizagem no decorrer desta unidade influenciaram suas respostas?
- O que você pode fazer para aprimorar ainda mais os conhecimentos adquiridos nesta unidade?
    a. Procurar conhecer mais sobre os alimentos adequados para cada refeição, bem como sobre diferentes hábitos saudáveis, que podem e devem ser incorporados em nosso cotidiano.
    b. Responder a diferentes *quizzes* sobre assuntos pessoais, identificando os elementos linguísticos mais comuns ao gênero.
    c. Aprofundar meus conhecimentos em língua inglesa, usando recursos diversos, de forma que minha participação nas atividades seja mais ativa.
    d. Outros.

UNIT 6

SPORTS AND YOU

Nesta unidade você terá oportunidade de:

- refletir e discutir sobre a importância da prática esportiva;
- reconhecer os objetivos e algumas características de perfis e elaborar um;
- escutar e compreender um programa de rádio sobre a importância da prática esportiva na adolescência;
- pesquisar sobre um esportista e expor oralmente as informações obtidas.

- Que relação podemos estabelecer entre as imagens e o título da unidade?
- Quais reflexões você acredita que a unidade irá lhe propor e de que forma elas poderão contribuir com seu cotidiano?
- Na sua opinião, as modalidades coletivas permitem o desenvolvimento de habilidades e competências mais relevantes do que as modalidades individuais?

Da esquerda para a direita, de cima para baixo: Andre Dib/Pulsar Imagens, João Prudente/Pulsar Imagens, Boris Streubel/Bongarts/Getty Images, Tom Dulat/Getty Images, William Volcov/Brazil Photo Press/LatinContent/Getty Images, Cesar Diniz/Pulsar Imagens

STARTING OUT

 Biology
Physical Education

1. Are these team or individual sports? Write T or I accordingly, in your notebook.
   a. football (US)
   b. baseball
   c. basketball
   d. curling
   e. cycling
   f. handball
   g. hang-gliding
   h. ice hockey
   i. judo
   j. martial arts
   k. rugby
   l. skiing
   m. soccer
   n. surfing
   o. swimming
   p. tennis
   q. triathlon
   r. volleyball
   s. water polo
   t. weightlifting

2. Answer the questions. Then work in pairs to compare your answers and report them to the class. Do you share the same interests?
   a. Do you prefer activities that you can do with your friends or by yourself? Justify your preference.
   b. What are your favorite sports to play?
   c. What are your favorite sports to watch on TV?
   d. Are winter sports as fun as summer sports? Why/Why not?
   e. What new sports would you like to try? Why?
   f. How do you feel about extreme sports?

3. Choose the best alternative to complete the statements.
   I get information about athletes or other famous people I admire by...
   - reading their online profiles.
   - interviewing them.
   - watching their performances.
   - writing them e-mails.
   - taking quizzes.

READING COMPREHENSION

Before Reading

1. Scan Beatriz Cunha's profile and answer the question: Where can you find information about her education?

Reading

CUNHA Beatriz

Sport	Shooting
NPC	Brazil
Gender	Women
Age	46
Place of Birth	São Paulo, BRA

Human Interest

Impairment Information

Classification	SH1

Further Personal Information

Residence	Palhoça, BRA
Occupation	Athlete
Language	Portuguese
Higher education	Food Technology – University of Barretos: São Paulo, BRA

Sport Specific Information

When and where did you begin this sport?	She began shooting in 2008.
Why this sport?	Having given up para-swimming she was feeling depressed and wanted to find another sport. She turned to the Association for Physically Disabled of Parana [ADFP]. "I looked at all the sports available, but it was in shooting that I found myself."
Club / Team	Florianopolitana Disability Association [AFLODEF]:
Name of coach	Fernando Cardoso [national]
Coach from which country?	Brazil

General Interest

Other sports	She competed in para-swimming, and is a former Brazilian national champion in open water. <portalctea.com.br> 07 Jul 2011.
Impairment	She was born with spina bifida. <portalctea.com.br> 07 Jul 2011.

Competition Highlights (historical)

World Championships

Rank	Year	Event	Result
31	2014	P2 - 10m Air Pistol SH1	337

Adapted from <www.paralympic.org/athletes/biographies>. Accessed on November 8, 2015.

2. Answer the questions in your notebook.

   a. What is Beatriz Cunha's impairment?

   b. What did she major in? Where?

   c. Was she successful as a para-swimming athlete? Justify your answer.

3. Read the text again and find the only true statement about Beatriz Cunha.

   a. She still does para-swimming.

   b. She is a self-taught shooter and doesn't need a coach.

   c. She has a congenital disability.

   d. She didn't compete in 2014.

4. Beatriz Cunha was depressed after giving up para-swimming, but she overcame depression when she found shooting. In pairs, discuss the questions below. Then write down your answers.

   a. Do you think the practice of sports can change a person's life? Explain.

   b. What benefits can the practice of sports bring to a disabled person?

5. Scan part of the Paralympic athlete Kamal Mammadov's profile and answer: What happened to him in 2005?

> **TIP**
> Algumas perguntas têm como respostas detalhes bem específicos e importantes. Procure reler o texto atentamente e selecione essas informações.

MAMMADOV Kamal

Sport	Wheelchair Dance Sport
NPC	Azerbaijan
Gender	Men
Place of Birth	Riga, LAT

Human Interest

Impairment Information

Origin of Impairment	Accident

Further Personal Information

Residence	Baku, AZE
Occupation	Athlete
Languages	Portuguese
Higher education	Law - Moscow State University: Moscow, RUS

General Interest

Other sports	He also competes in wheelchair fencing. (http://paralympic.az, 2 Dec 2013)
Impairment	He lost the ability to walk after a car accident in 2005. "My life began when I sat in the wheelchair. It has become much more beautiful and colourful than before." (bizimyolinfo.com, 3 Jul 2013; vestnikkavkaza.net, 11 June 2013)

Adapted from <www.paralympic.org/athletes/biographies>. Accessed on November 8, 2015.

Unit 6 Sports and You

6. Read Mammadov's quote. Then discuss the questions below in small groups.

   > "My life began when I sat in the wheelchair. It has become much more beautiful and colourful than before."

   a. What do you understand from the quote?

   b. In your opinion, how important is a positive attitude in overcoming difficulties, challenges, and temporary setbacks in life? Explain your view.

7. You have read the profiles of two Paralympic athletes. You can find more profiles at the website <www.paralympic.org>. Reflect on the questions below and answer them.

   a. Why do you think more profiles are available there?

   b. Who would be interested in reading them?

   c. Would you like to know more about Paralympic athletes? Why?

8. Match the two sets of sentences to form some characteristics of profiles.

   a. Profiles are

   b. The language can be

   c. They include pieces of information about

   d. Information is organized in topics

   e. People create profiles

   1. formal or informal depending on the target audience.

   2. concise.

   3. in order to make the reading easier and faster.

   4. personal life, career, achievements, skills, and interests.

   5. to do things like join social networks, look for a job, or publish their achievements.

After Reading

- Is playing sports important to you? Justify your answer.
- We know that sports benefit our lives. Do you think that sports can have a negative side as well? Explain.
- Are there any public places in your community where people can play sports? If so, how could you improve these places? Why? If not, how would sports centers benefit your community? Justify your answer.

VOCABULARY STUDY

1. Read the statements extracted from the profile on page 95. Match the phrasal verbs in bold to their definitions. There are two extra alternatives.

   a. "Having **given up** para-swimming she was feeling depressed and wanted to find another sport."

   b. "She **turned to** the Association for Physically Disabled of Parana [ADFP]."

   - Go to for help, advice, or information
   - Prepare for physical exertion or a performance by exercising or practicing gently beforehand
   - Cease making an effort; resign oneself to failure
   - Cease to participate in a race or competition

   Extracted from <www.oxforddictionaries.com/us>. Accessed on November 9, 2015.

2. Use one of the phrasal verbs from the previous activity to complete the quote below. Then discuss it with a classmate.

   > "A true champion is someone who wants to make a difference, who never ♦, and who gives everything she has no matter what the circumstances are. A true champion works hard and never loses sight of her dreams." (Dot Richardson, American softball player)

   Extracted from <www.motivational-inspirational-corner.com/getquote.html?categoryid=254>. Accessed on March 29, 2016.

3. The words *sport*, *classification*, *information*, and *residence* from the profile on page 95 are cognates. Scan the text for five other cognates and write them in your notebook.

   > Palavras cognatas ou transparentes têm significado e grafia parecidos em duas línguas.

4. Use the information from the box to complete the *Sports Collocations* chart below.

   > Collocations são duas ou mais palavras que geralmente são usadas juntas em inglês.

   hockey   karate   sailing   skiing   squash
   table tennis   taekwondo   windsurfing   yoga

play	do	go
badminton	gymnastics	cycling
hockey	judo	jogging
♦	♦	♦
♦	♦	♦
♦	♦	♦

Unit 6 Sports and You

LANGUAGE IN CONTEXT

Simple Past

1. Read the following extracts from the profile on page 95 and choose the correct options to complete the sentences.

   > "She **began** shooting in 2008."
   >
   > "Having given up para-swimming she was feeling depressed and **wanted** to find another sport. She **turned** to the Association for Physically Disabled of Parana [ADFP]. "I **looked** at all the sports available, but it **was** in shooting that I **found** myself.""
   >
   > "She **competed** in para-swimming, and is a former Brazilian national champion in open water. (portalctea.com.br, 7 Jul 2011)"
   >
   > "She **was born** with spina bifida. (portalctea.com.br, 7 Jul 2011)"

   a. The verbs in bold express states, actions, and events that…

   - will happen in the future.
   - happened in a specific time in the past.

   b. *Want*, *turn*, ♦, and *compete* are regular verbs. Regular verbs end in ♦ in the Simple Past.

   - look/*ed*
   - be/*ing*

   c. *Begin*, *be*, ♦ , and *be born* are ♦ verbs because they don't follow any specific rules in the Simple Past.

   - turn/regular
   - find/irregular

2. Based on the extracts in activity 1, pick out the correct answers to the following questions.

   a. **Did** Beatriz **begin** shooting in 2005?
   - No, she **didn't**. She **began** shooting in 2008.
   - Yes, she **did**. She **began** in December, 2005.

   b. Why **did** Beatriz **want** to find another sport?
   - Because she **was** depressed.
   - Because she **wanted** to swim.

   c. In which sport **did** Beatriz **find** herself?
   - She **found** herself in all the sports available.
   - She **found** herself in shooting.

Sports and You **Unit 6**   99

3. Pay attention to the highlighted verb structures in activities 1 and 2. Then select the correct alternatives to complete the rules for the Simple Past.

   a. We use the Simple Past to talk about *finished / unfinished* actions, states, or events in a specific time in the past.

   b. In affirmative sentences, we use the *base / past* form of the verbs. In interrogative sentences, we use *did / does* + subject + main verb in the base form. In negative statements, we use subject + did not (didn't) + main verb in the *past / base* form.

   c. For short answers, we use Yes / No + *subject / main verb* + *did / didn't*.

   d. *Was* and *were* are the past forms of the verb *to have / to be*. *Was* is used when the subjects are I, he, she, and it. *Were* is used when the subjects are we, you, and they.

   For spelling rules of regular and irregular verbs, refer to Language Reference, page 176 and the Irregular Verbs List, page 189.

4. Read part of a testimony written by someone whose life was turned around by exercise. Choose the best alternative to complete it.

   After struggling with depression, exercise turned my life around. Here's how I learned to love the gym.

   […]

   We all hear that exercise is vital to overcoming depression. Great. I ♦(1) myself to go running or lift weights, was extremely bored during longer runs, and ♦(2) more tired afterwards than I was before. I just assumed that my body was not meant to handle exercise, and I envied those people who ♦(3) full of energy and ♦(4) in great shape.

   Then, one day, I ♦(5) to try something new. I ♦(6) that exercise was important, but I knew I couldn't maintain a schedule of something I ♦(7) doing. Seeing as how I ♦(8) in the middle of an interesting novel, I decided to bring that book with me and read while I ♦(9) some light pedaling on the stationary bike. I figured this wouldn't really do much in terms of exercise because I ♦(10) the resistance way down and I wasn't pushing as hard as I could. So I ended up reading for a bit; I could tell that my heart rate was up, but I never really ♦(11) out of breath. Before I knew it I had finished two chapters, 30 minutes had gone by and I was drenched in sweat. And I ♦(12) great! It was honestly the first time I had enjoyed working out.

   […]

   Extracted from <www.reddit.com/r/Fitness/comments/18t2f6/after_struggling_with_depression_exercise_turned/>. Accessed on June 19, 2015.

   - forced - ended up - seemed - didn't - didn't decide - knew - enjoyed - were - didn't - had - didn't get - fell
   - forced - ended up - seemed - were - decided - knew - didn't enjoy - were - did - didn't have - got - fell
   - forced - ended up - seemed - were - decided - knew - didn't enjoy - was - did - had - got - felt

100 Unit 6 Sports and You

5. Complete the text using the verbs from the box in the Simple Past.

> anchor   become   confirm   create   defend
> help   lower   realize   smash   stay   win

[...]
Arguably the most naturally gifted athlete the world has ever seen, Usain St Leo Bolt, (1) ♦ his tremendous talents when he (2) ♦ his dreams by winning a phenomenal three gold medals and breaking three world records at the 2008 Olympic Games in Beijing, China. Bolt (3) ♦ the first man in Olympic history to win both the 100m and 200m races in world record times and then as part of the 4x100m team that also (4) ♦ the world record later in the meet. He (5) ♦ history again and became a legend at the 2012 Olympic Games in London by defending all three Olympic titles with 100m, 200m and 4x100m victories, the latter in a new world record time of 36.84 secs.

Between his Olympic successes Usain (6) ♦ firmly in the global spotlight winning three gold medals and setting two individual world records at the 2009 IAAF World T&F Championships in Berlin, Germany. He (7) ♦ his 100m time to a staggering 9.58 secs, his 200m time to 19.19 secs and running the third leg (8) ♦ Jamaica to gold in the 4x100m. He (9) ♦ his World Championships title in the 200m at the 2011 IAAF World T&F Championships in Daegu, Korea and (10) ♦ Jamaica to another world record of 37.04 secs in the 4x100m. In 2013 at the IAAF World T&F Championships in Moscow Usain (11) ♦ the 100m, 200m and 4x100m to make it 8 World Championship gold medals.
[...]

Extracted from <usainbolt.com/bio/>. Accessed on June 19, 2015.

WRAPPING UP

In pairs, read the extract about the Indian athlete Khushbir Kaur and reread Bolt's biography in activity 5. Then decide which athlete each of you is going to work on. In your notebook, write three questions about him/her using the Simple Past. Then ask your classmate those questions. Change roles.

India's Hopes Riding On These Athletes At The 2016 Rio Olympics

[...]

Khushbir Kaur (Women's 20 km walk)

Born in Amritsar, Khushbir Kaur, 22, reached a personal best of 1:33:07 during the 2014 Asian championships in Japan, setting a new national record. In the 2015 World Championships, she came 37th after clocking 1:38:53 in the 20km walk. She has earned the one quota place for the Rio Games.

[...]

Adapted from <www.indiatimes.com/news/sports/indias-hopes-riding-on-these-athletes-at-the-2016-rio-olympics-244524.html>. Accessed on November 9, 2015.

LISTENING COMPREHENSION

Before Listening

1. Listen to the introduction of a radio program and choose the correct answer to the question: What is the focus of today's program?

- The importance of routine physical activity in teens' lives.
- The importance of daily brain exercises in teens' lives.
- The importance of Physical Education classes for teens.

Listening

2. Now listen to another part of the program and number the paragraphs in the order you hear them.

- Both girls are on the Bogota High School volleyball team in northern New Jersey. And their experience gaining confidence and winning friends illustrates just what researchers in the Netherlands found when they surveyed 7,000 Dutch students between the ages of 11 and 16. The study appeared in the journal "Clinical Psychological Science". Yale University child psychologist Alan Kazdin is editor. He says the findings show just how bountiful the benefits of exercise can be.

- I really don't care what other people think anymore. So, I can be myself around anyone. And I think a lot of people I've grown friendships with them because I really like myself.

- I think it'd be too strong to call it an elixir, but it has the broad effects of something like that.

- In the study, teenagers who took part in organized sports had a more positive self-image, and greater self-esteem than teens who weren't physically active. They were simply happier, says Kazdin, more grounded, and less likely to engage in problematic behavior.

- I've made something of myself, I feel. I feel like I'm not just like everyone else. Like, we all work hard to be something and like, it pays off and people recognize it. So it feels good.

- Researchers found physical activity can help teenagers in two powerful ways. One is confidence. Take 16-year-old volleyball player Jennifer Ramirez.

- Then there's sociability - friends. Here's 17-year-old teammate Carly O'Sullivan.

After Listening

Which photo best represents the results of the research from the Netherlands? Why? Talk to your classmates.

a.

b.

13 PRONUNCIATION PRACTICE

Final ed sound
Listen to the following verbs and pay attention to their corresponding final sound.

a.	wanted	**/id/**	/d/	/t/
b.	closed	/id/	**/d/**	/t/
c.	worked	/id/	/d/	**/t/**

Now listen to these verbs and identify the correct alternative.

d.	appeared	/id/	/d/	/t/
e.	cleaned	/id/	/d/	/t/
f.	started	/id/	/d/	/t/
g.	looked	/id/	/d/	/t/
h.	watched	/id/	/d/	/t/

SPEAKING

Think of an athlete you admire and research about him/her in magazines or on the Internet.
- ✓ You can take notes in your notebook to help you, if necessary.
- ✓ Work in pairs. Ask a classmate as many questions as possible and try to find out who your classmate researched. Take turns.
- ✓ Make sure you use the language studied in this unit appropriately.

WRITING

In small groups, follow the steps below and create a profile of a person you admire.

Planning your profile

- Exchange ideas about the person you admire the most. He/She can be a famous person from the entertainment business, sports, politics, or someone from your community.
- Do some research and gather information about his/her personal life, achievements, and skills.

Writing and rewriting your text

- Use the information you've gathered and write a draft of the profile in your notebook.

> **REFLECTING AND EVALUATING**
>
> Go back to your profile and make sure you paid enough attention to the following topics:
> - ✓ Is the language appropriate to your target audience?
> - ✓ Is the text concise?
> - ✓ Is there information about achievements, skills, interests, and other things?
> - ✓ Is the profile organized by topics?

- Exchange profiles with a classmate and ask for his/her opinions and suggestions.
- Write it on a sheet of paper or cardboard, making all the necessary changes.
- If possible, paste a picture of the person you wrote about.

After writing

- Gather the profiles of the people you and your classmates admire the most and make a mural.
- If possible, publish it on the school website or on a wall in the school.
- Invite students, teachers, and school staff to visit the mural and read the profiles.

SELF-ASSESSMENT

Chegamos ao fim da unidade 6. Convidamos você a refletir sobre seu desempenho até aqui e responder às questões propostas abaixo, escolhendo uma das seguintes opções:

Sim.

Preciso me preparar mais.

Questões

- Você adquiriu repertório suficiente para discutir e posicionar-se criticamente sobre a importância da prática esportiva?
- Você se considera apto a ler e compreender diferentes perfis e reconhecer as características principais inerentes ao gênero?
- Você reúne conhecimentos linguístico-discursivos suficientes para produzir um perfil em língua inglesa?
- Você se sente preparado para escutar e compreender programas de rádios sobre a prática esportiva na adolescência?
- Você se julga apto a fazer perguntas aos seus colegas acerca de um esportista e descobrir quem ele é?

Refletindo sobre suas respostas

- Como você analisa a evolução do seu aprendizado em relação à unidade anterior?
- De que forma suas práticas de aprendizagem no decorrer desta unidade influenciaram suas respostas?
- O que você pode fazer para aprimorar ainda mais os conhecimentos adquiridos nesta unidade?
    - **a.** Buscar mais informações sobre a importância da prática esportiva para todos, em especial sobre os benefícios que ela traz para os adolescentes.
    - **b.** Ler perfis de diferentes esportistas e identificar os elementos lexicais e linguísticos mais comumente usados.
    - **c.** Aprofundar meus conhecimentos em língua inglesa, usando recursos diversos, de forma que minha participação nas atividades seja mais ativa.
    - **d.** Outros.

Further Practice 3 – Units 5 & 6

1. Read the cartoons and the statements below. Then number the statements accordingly in your notebook.

Extracted from <www.glasbergen.com/?count=1&s=restaurant>. Accessed on June 29, 2015.

Extracted from <www.glasbergen.com/search/cartoons+on+health/?count=29>. Accessed on June 29, 2015.

a. The mother is concerned about her son's eating habits.

b. The mother really wants him to eat healthy food.

c. Junk food makes people fat.

d. The son is trying to confuse his mother, so he doesn't have to eat what she offers him.

e. The mother is aware that junk food isn't a good thing to eat.

2. Most people know that junk food is unhealthy and has little nutritional value. In your opinion, why do so many people eat it?

3. Read the text and write T (True) or F (False).

Characteristics of eating culture in Japan

Isao Kumakura
President, Shizuoka University of Art and Culture
Director, Hayashibara Museum of Art

Roots in the natural environment

Japan is a long island – about 3,500 km in length from north-east to south-west, situated in the Pacific Ocean to the east of the Eurasian bloc. The surrounding sea is a mixture of warm and cold streams, giving abundant varieties of fish. The Japanese climate is characterized by warm monsoons, although the northern region is temperate and the southern islands subtropical.

As a result, distinct changes over four seasons are experienced, which has been an important factor in Japanese cuisine. There are two rainy seasons in Japan. One is in June (Tsuyu: "plum rain") and the other is in September (Akisame: autumn rain). The annual rainfall averages 2,000 mm, so fresh water is abundant. This water provides benefits to Japanese agriculture, allowing cultivation of rice, vegetables and fruit. Thanks to its widespread availability, extensive water use is characteristic of Japanese cuisine. About 70% of the land in Japan is mountainous, with very few plains. The mountains are covered with deep forest. [...]

Raw ingredients

A primary characteristic of Japanese cuisine is the enjoyment of the raw taste of food, without using strongly-flavoured sauces. Typical examples are sashimi (raw fish slices) and sushi (vinegared rice topped with raw fish). Sashimi is prepared simply by cutting fresh fish. Freshness is ensured by various methods and hygiene is carefully maintained. Cutting methods were also developed specifically to maintain good taste. The knife used to cut sashimi is a long knife beveled on one side. The sharpness of the edge and the slicing method involves pulling the knife on the fish, which does not damage the tissues, maintaining its umami (savouriness). [...]

Extracted from <www8.cao.go.jp/syokuiku/data/eng_pamph/pdf/pamph5.pdf>. Accessed on November 8, 2015.

Further Practice 3 – Units 5 & 6

   a. Due to its location, there is a great variety of fish in Japan.

   b. Japan suffers from a shortage of fresh water.

   c. Japanese people like raw seafood such as sashimi and sushi.

   d. It's easy to make sashimi.

4. Answer the questions.

   a. Have you ever tried Japanese food? If so, did you like it? If not, would you like to? Why?

   b. Are you open to trying new food? Why/Why not?

5. Complete the text about the Brazilian Paralympic athlete Terezinha Guilhermina with the past tense forms of the verbs in the box.

> be   join   say   win

Usain Bolt guides Brazil's Terezinha Guilhermina

• Date: 21-04-2015

• Related to: Athletics

Brazil's three-time Paralympic sprinting champion Terezinha Guilhermina unveiled her new guide on Saturday (18 April) in Rio de Janeiro, Brazil – none other than Jamaica's six-time Olympic champion Usain Bolt!

Bolt (1) ♦ in the host city of next year's Olympic and Paralympic Games to promote the Mano a Mano Challenge at the Brazilian Jockey Club and, grinning all the way, (2) ♦ with blind athlete Guilhermina to take part in a 50m sprint.

"It was a dream come true," said Guilhermina, who (3) ♦ 100m and 200m gold at the London 2012 Games and 200m gold at the Beijing 2008 Games. "He was a little uncertain at the start, afraid that I might fall over or that he would run too fast. This shows how much respect events like this bring to Paralympic athletes."

"Running with him [Bolt] is a joy for any athlete. Bolt is a reference in the sport and I'm happy to have participated in this race. I fulfilled a dream."

Guilhermina has plenty on her schedule this year. "I have the Parapan American Games (in Toronto in August) and then the World Championships in Doha (in October)," she (4) ♦. "So it will be a very important year in terms of preparations for the Rio 2016 Games."

[...]

Extracted from <www.ibsasport.org/news/713/usain-bolt-guides-brazils-terezinha-guilhermina>. Accessed on June 29, 2015.

6. Write F (Fact) or UF (Unknown Fact) according to the text.

   a. Terezinha Guilhermina has won three gold medals at Paralympic Games.

   b. Terezinha has also won some bronze medals in international competitions.

   c. In Guilhermina's opinion, Usain Bolt is a reference in running.

   d. Usain Bolt and Terezinha Guilhermina became friends.

   e. Terezinha is visually impaired.

7. Choose the parts that justify the statements below.

   a. Terezinha Guilhermina is a fan of Usain Bolt.
   - This shows how much respect events like this bring to Paralympic athletes. […]
   - "It was a dream come true," said Guilhermina, […]

   b. The Jamaican athlete is a very friendly person.
   - […] grinning all the way, joined with blind athlete Guilhermina […]
   - Bolt was in the host city of next year's Olympic and Paralympic Games to promote the Mano a Mano Challenge […]

8. Answer the questions.

   a. What do you think about what Usain Bolt did for Terezinha Guilhermina?

   b. Have you ever personally met someone you admire? If so, tell about your experience. If not, would you like to? Why?

9. Read the quote below and answer the questions that follow.

"The important thing in life is not to triumph but to compete."

(Pierre de Coubertin, French educator and historian)

Extracted from <www.brainyquote.com/quotes/authors/p/pierre_de_coubertin.html#8271mX7ljsHlfHT2.99. Accessed on March 31, 2016.

Cobertin is considered the father of the modern Olympic Games. Do you think that his quote can be related only to sports competitions? Why/Why not?

Further Practice 3 – Units 5 & 6

10. Read the text below and work in pairs to discuss the questions.

Khel Khel Mein – Transforming The Lives of Underprivileged Kids Using Sports!

Akshai Abraham had a dream – of helping marginalized children reach their true potential with the help of sports. Read about his brilliant organization in Lucknow, which is doing just that – using sports in empowering underprivileged youth and improving their life prospects, besides imparting life skills to them and reviving traditional sports on the brink of extinction!

Nelson Mandela, the legendary South African activist and politician, identified the transformative and unifying power of sports and used that power to build a nation which otherwise protests and diplomacy could not. 'Sport has the power to change the world', Mandela said. These were indeed the exact thoughts of Akshai Abraham, the founder of ProjectKHEL.

Akshai Abraham is an MBA from the prestigious Indian Institute of Forest Management (IIFM), Bhopal. He has over 7 years of experience including 6 years in the social sector in the areas of research, program development, project management and organization building and also a year's international experience as a cultural exchange intern in Austria. In 2001-2002, as he worked in Austria for about a year as an AIESEC trainee, his experience of living and working in a highly developed country motivated him to rethink his career plans from IT to the social sector. A keen sportsman and a committed non-profit professional, Akshai's vision is to impact the lives of underprivileged children and youth of India through KHEL. Says he:

> My school education had a lot of focus on sports and extra-curricular activities. Sports played a big role in shaping my character and help me deal with many problems and difficulties including the early demise of my father. Sport has stayed with me throughout my life. Though never a really competitive sportsman, I played all sports whenever there was a chance and it helped me make friends, relieve stress, connect with colleagues and peers in a unique manner. Thus while the idea of starting a sports related program for children had been lingering for years, the idea of implementing Project KHEL was probably planted sometime in 2009-10. In 2012, after having worked in the development sector for 6-7 years, I felt the time was right to start my own initiative and Project KHEL came into being. […]

Adapted from <www.thebetterindia.com/9149/khel-khel-mein-transforming-lives-underprivileged-kids-using-sports/>.
Accessed on November 8, 2015.

a. Nelson Mandela said "Sport has the power to change the world". Do you think this is true? Justify your answer.

b. What is your opinion of Akshai Abraham's initiative?

c. Akshai Abraham said that sports helped him to overcome difficulties in life. Do you think sports can have this much power over people?

EXAM PRACTICE

Alongamentos são atividades que promovem o estiramento das fibras musculares e, consequentemente, aumentam a flexibilidade muscular. Com base no texto e na atividade mostrada pela imagem, pode-se inferir que:

a. O alongamento apresentado na imagem causa bem-estar por motivos não comprovados cientificamente.

b. Caso as orientações para o alongamento não sejam seguidas corretamente, o efeito pode ser diametralmente oposto ao desejado.

c. Somente a observação da imagem permite que o leitor repita o movimento e alcance completamente os resultados desejados.

d. A atividade de alongamento, quando executada em conjunto com outros recursos, pode ter seus efeitos maximizados.

e. Atividades de alongamento como a descrita no artigo devem ser feitas apenas de maneira assistida.

UNIT 7

YOU DON'T NEED THAT MUCH

Nesta unidade você terá oportunidade de:

- refletir e discutir sobre o excesso de consumo na atualidade e seus efeitos;

- reconhecer os objetivos e algumas características de anúncios publicitários e criar um;

- escutar e compreender uma letra de música sobre a relação entre a sociedade e o consumismo;

- analisar informações específicas em um infográfico, fazer uma pesquisa e comparar oralmente as informações obtidas com as analisadas.

- O que podemos ver na imagem? Quais os elementos em evidência?

- Qual relação podemos estabelecer entre a imagem e o título da unidade?

- O que você entende por consumidor e consumista?

STARTING OUT

1. Work in pairs to match the products or companies to their corresponding slogans.

   a. Think different.

   b. Priceless.

   c. I'm lovin' it.

   d. Just do it.

   e. Melts in your mouth, not in your hand.

   f. Open Happiness.

   - McDonald's
   - Mastercard
   - Coca-Cola
   - M&M's
   - Apple Inc.
   - Nike

2. In groups of three, read the quote and discuss the questions below. Then report and justify your answers to the class.

   > "We buy things we don't need with money we don't have to impress people we don't like." (Dave Ramsey, American author and radio host)
   >
   > Extracted from <www.goodreads.com/quotes/25775-we-buy-things-we-don-t-need-with-money-we-don-t>. Accessed on June 21, 2015.

   a. Why do you think we buy things we don't need?

   b. Would it make a big difference in your life if you changed your spending habits? Why do you think so?

   c. Have you ever bought anything because of an advertisement? If so, which aspect of the ad persuaded you?

   d. Do you often associate products to the celebrities who advertise them? Do certain celebrities make you want or not want to buy a product?

   e. Are you for or against advertisement-free zones? Why?

3. Complete the sentences below in your notebook. Afterwards, discuss them with your classmates.

   a. In my opinion, ad campaigns have to ♦.

   b. Advertising is efficiently persuasive when ♦.

   c. An ad campaign that caught my attention was ♦.

READING COMPREHENSION

Before Reading

1. Look at the advertisement below and answer: Which product is being advertised? Where is it being advertised? What kind of information do you think you'll find in this ad?

> **TIP**
> Lembre-se de que, ao fazer previsões e inferências, os seus conhecimentos prévios e de mundo são acionados. Levante hipóteses e estabeleça conexões com o texto a ser lido. Isso, certamente, facilitará a sua compreensão.

Reading

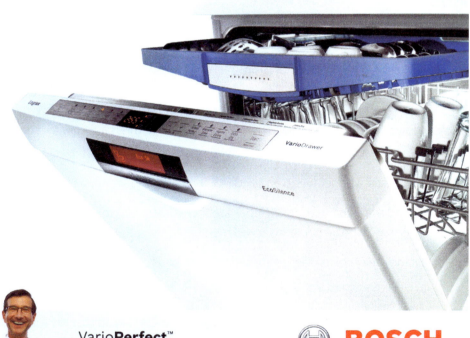

Extracted from GOOD HOMES Magazine, page 139. November, 2015.

2. Choose the true sentences about the ad.

   a. The dishwasher manufacturer is not mentioned in the ad.

   b. There is a website where people can get more information about the product.

   c. Housewives are the target audience of the ad.

   d. The dishwasher, not Karl, is the focus of the ad.

3. Logotypes and slogans are powerful and visible symbols of a company. Read the definition of both words and identify Bosch's logo and slogan. Then answer the questions that follow: Do you think that slogans and logotypes can really influence consumers? Why/Why not?

   Slogan
   A word or phrase that is easy to remember and is used by a group or business to attract attention

   Extracted from <www.merriam-webster.com/dictionary/slogan>. Accessed on March 31, 2016.

   Logotype
   An identifying symbol (as for use in advertising)

   Extracted from <www.merriam-webster.com/dictionary/logotype>. Accessed on March 31, 2016.

   a. Invented for life.

   b. BOSCH

4. Go back to the ad on page 115 and identify a word that is not in English. Then answer: Which word is that? Why do you think that word was used? Do you believe this is an effective strategy? Why/Why not?

5. In pairs, discuss these questions about the ad on page 115. Then write the answers in you notebook.

   a. Besides the logo and the slogan, the ad includes another reference to the manufacturer. Which reference is that? Why do you think it was mentioned?

   b. Do you think that the use of colors plays an important role in purchasing and branding? Justify.

   c. In your opinion, were colors used well in this ad? Why?

   d. From your view, why does the manufacturer refer to the engineer? Do ads usually make use of characters or famous people? Why?

   e. Do you think that dishwashers are essential to our lives? Why?

   f. In your opinion, who would be interested in buying a dishwasher like the one in the ad? Explain.

   g. The company says people can have energy savings of up to 39% if they use the dishwasher in the ad. Is energy something consumers should pay attention to when buying a product? Justify your answer.

> Algumas palavras em inglês são comumente usadas em língua portuguesa. Tratam-se de estrangeirismos, ou seja, palavras e expressões emprestadas de outro idioma. A palavra *slogan*, por exemplo, é muito utilizada na linguagem relacionada à publicidade.

6. Read the advertisement below and answer the questions.

Extracted from <www.vintageadbrowser.com/electronics-ads-1950s>. Accessed on November 13, 2015.

   a. What do this advertisement and the one on page 115 have in common? What are their differences?

   b. Which visual elements suggest that this advertisement is from the 1950's?

7. Find the only sentence that is not true about the characteristics of advertisements.

   a. The language focuses on the target audience.

   b. Advertisements usually count on appealing images.

   c. They never have logos.

   d. The objective of ads is to advertise a product, a service, or an idea.

   e. Ads usually have a tagline or a slogan.

After Reading

- How do advertisements increase consumerism?
- Are you influenced by advertisements when you want to buy something? If so, do you think this influence is positive or negative? Explain.
- What are the consequences of advertising for people who buy compulsively?

VOCABULARY STUDY

1. Refer to the ad on page 115 to infer the meaning of the words or expressions in the box. Next use them to complete the passages below.

   > Falsos cognatos, também conhecidos como falsos amigos (*false friends*), são palavras semelhantes na forma escrita, mas que têm sentidos diferentes em duas línguas.

   clean   dishwasher   find out   save   VarioSpeed

   a. 6 ways to save time on everyday household tasks

   […]

   The days of hand washing are gone. Most modern houses are now equipped with a ♦₍₁₎, some even have two! And with a good reason. According to one study, the average dishwasher uses just 16% of the water that hand washing uses. Not to mention the obvious time saving benefits! Bosch dishwashers ₍₂₎♦ time and water, while also delivering perfectly ₍₃₎♦ dishes. Their ₍₄₎♦ technology cleans dishes in half the time of a conventional dishwasher. […]

   Adapted from <www.independent.ie/life/smart-consumer/6-ways-to-save-time-on-every-day-household-tasks-31114466.html>. Accessed on November 10, 2015.

   b. Does subliminal advertising actually work?

   Hidden messages that promote products in films once caused a moral panic. But is the much-feared technique really effective? The BBC's Phil Tinline helped devise an experiment to ₍₅₎♦. […]

   Extracted from <www.bbc.com/news/magazine-30878843>. Accessed on November 10, 2015.

2. In the question "Does subliminal advertising **actually** work?", extracted from activity 1, the word in bold is a false cognate. What does it mean?

   - at present
   - really
   - at the moment

3. Below is a list of false cognates. Match them to their correct meanings.

a. college	**c.** legend	**e.** lunch	**g.** pretend
b. costume	**d.** library	**f.** parent	**h.** push

   - A father or mother.
   - A set of clothes worn by an actor or other performer for a particular role or by someone attending a masquerade.
   - One providing higher education or specialized professional or vocational training.
   - Speak and act so as to make it appear that something is the case when in fact it is not.
   - Exert force on (someone or something), typically with one's hand, in order to move them away from oneself or the origin of the force.
   - A traditional story sometimes popularly regarded as historical but unauthenticated.
   - A meal eaten in the middle of the day, typically one that is lighter or less formal than an evening meal.
   - A building or room containing collections of books, periodicals, and sometimes films and recorded music for people to read, borrow, or refer to.

   Extracted from <www.oxforddictionaries.com/>. Accessed on June 22, 2015.

LANGUAGE IN CONTEXT

Modal Verbs *Can*, *May*, and *Could*

1. Read this excerpt from the ad on page 115 and look for the correct answer to the question: What does the word in bold indicate in context?

   "Today, our latest dishwashers come with VarioPerfect™, so now you **can** choose to save time or more energy."

   a. ability

   b. permission

   c. possibility

TIP

Lembre-se de que uma mesma palavra pode expressar diferentes sentidos de acordo com o contexto em que ela está inserida.

2. Put the words in the box in the correct order and complete the ad below. Write in your notebook.

   celebrate   do   than   You   can   more

Extracted from <theinspirationroom.com/daily/2009/amnesty-international-cakes/>. Accessed on November 11, 2015.

You Don't Need that Much **Unit 7**

3. Now read another ad and find two modal verb forms which express an idea that is contrary to the one conveyed in activities 1 and 2 from page 119.

Extracted from *Teen Vogue*. Back cover – August, 2014

4. Refer to the ads in the previous activities and choose the correct answer to the question. Where are modal verbs often positioned?

   • After the base form of other verbs.

   • Before the base form of other verbs.

5. Now reread the bottom left information from the ad in activity 3 and choose the correct alternatives to complete the sentences.

   "Check out what **could** be forming under the surface at…"

   a. In the excerpt above, *could* expresses a *weak possibility / strong prohibition*.

   b. The *interrogative / negative* form of *could* is *could not* or *couldn't*.

   For other uses of the modals can, could, and may, refer to Language Reference, page 178.

120 Unit 7 You Don't Need that Much

6. Use the verb combinations from the box to complete the quotes about advertising and consumerism.

> can drive   can have   can violate   cannot control
> could be   could talk   may not be   may seen

a. "We were the first people to do advertising on the Web. I actually saw in 1993 that the ad ♦ the content, the destination." (Tim O'Reilly, Irish businessman)

Extracted from <www.brainyquote.com/quotes/quotes/t/timoreill671270.html>.
Accessed on November 11, 2015.

b. "Patent monopoly creates a lot of problems. It allows the patentee to charge the maximum to consumers. This ♦ a problem if the patented product is a luxury item, like parts that go into a smartphone, but ♦ basic human rights if it involves things such as life-saving drugs." (Ha-Joon Chang, South Korean economist)

Extracted from <www.brainyquote.com/quotes/quotes/h/hajooncha694438.html>.
Accessed on June 22, 2015.

c. "Production chains, how consumers ♦ change: all these things ♦ at odds with fashion, but arguably, they're not." (Lily Cole, English actress)

Extracted from <www.brainyquote.com/quotes/quotes/l/lilycole603930.html>.
Accessed on November 11, 2015.

d. "Advertising, music, atmospheres, subliminal messages and films ♦ an impact on our emotional life, and we ♦ it because we are not even conscious of it." (Tariq Ramadan, Swiss writer)

Extracted from <www.brainyquote.com/quotes/quotes/t/tariqramad531501.html>.
Accessed on November 11, 2015.

e. "Advertising is salesmanship mass produced. No one would bother to use advertising if he ♦ to all his prospects face-to-face. But he can't." (Morris Hite, American businessman)

Extracted from <www.brainyquote.com/quotes/quotes/m/morrishite102981.html>. Accessed on November 11, 2015.

WRAPPING UP

In your notebook, write creative endings for the sentences below. Be careful with the meaning you want to express using the modal verbs in bold. Then share your thoughts with a classmate and report the best ideas to the class.

Advertising language **can** ♦.

Compulsive buyers **could** ♦.

Messages conveyed through ad campaigns **may** ♦.

LISTENING COMPREHENSION

Before Listening

1. You are going to listen to a song performed by Eddie Vedder. Have you ever heard of him? Do you know any of his songs? Share what you know with your classmates.

Listening

 2. Read the definitions of the words below and then use them to complete the lyrics of the song. One word is in a slightly different form in the song.

bleed: Lose blood from the body as a result of injury or illness

breed: A sort or kind of person or thing

greed: Intense and selfish desire for something, especially wealth, power, or food

keep: Continue or cause to continue in a specified condition, position, course etc.

Extracted from <www.oxforddictionaries.com>. Accessed on June 21, 2015.

Society
(originally by Jerry Hannan)

It's a mystery to me
We have a (1) ♦ with which we have agreed
And you think you have to want more than you need
Until you have it all, you won't be free

Society, you're a crazy (2) ♦
I hope you're not lonely without me

When you want more than you have, you think you need
And when you think more than you want, your thoughts begin to (3) ♦
I think I need to find a bigger place
Cause when you have more than you think, you need more space

Society, you're a crazy breed
I hope you're not lonely without me
Society, crazy indeed
Hope you're not lonely without me

There's those thinking more or less, less is more
But if less is more, how you (4) ♦ score?
Means for every point you make your level drops
Kinda like you're startin' from the top
And you can't do that

Society, you're a crazy breed
I hope you're not lonely without me
Society, crazy indeed
I hope you're not lonely without me
Society, have mercy on me
I hope you're not angry if I disagree
Society, you're crazy indeed
I hope you're not lonely without me

Extracted from <www.azlyrics.com/lyrics/eddievedder/society.html>. Accessed on September 5, 2015.

> **TIP**
> Não se preocupe em entender toda a letra da música. Preste atenção nas palavras-chave e observe o contexto para inferir o significado das palavras desconhecidas.

After Listening

Discuss these questions with your classmates.

- According to the song, what is the relationship between society and consumerism?
- What can you infer from the following lines?

    "There's those thinking more or less, less is more

    But if less is more, how you keepin score"

- In your view, what are the author's feelings towards people who consume more than necessary?

SPEAKING

In groups, have an informal conversation with your classmates about receptiveness to advertising on mobile devices.

✓ Read the infographic and identify the information that you believe is interesting.

✓ Do a research about similar information in the Brazilian market.

✓ Compare and contrast the information you collected with the ones provided by the infographic.

Adapted from <www.searchenginejournal.com/consumers-receptive-mobile-ads-study-shows-mobile-ad-engagement-increasing/113003/>. Accessed on June 21, 2015.

WRITING

In pairs, follow the steps below to create an advertisement.

Planning your ad

- Talk to your classmate and create a product to advertise or an idea to promote.
- Come up with a logo and an attractive slogan.
- Choose your target audience and decide where the ad will be published.
- Decide what images will be used to provoke a reaction in your target audience.

Writing and rewriting your text

- Write a draft and sketch your ad in your notebook.

> **REFLECTING AND EVALUATING**
>
> Go back to your ad and make sure you paid attention to the following topics:
>
> ✓ Is the language persuasive and appropriate to the audience?
>
> ✓ Does the slogan sound exciting and attractive?
>
> ✓ Are the images appealing?

- Show the draft to the teacher and to some classmates. Ask for their opinions.
- Make all the necessary adjustments.
- Write it out on a sheet of paper.

After writing

- Present your ad to the whole class and see how many of them would actually buy the product you have created or would follow the idea you have promoted.

SELF-ASSESSMENT

Chegamos ao fim da unidade 7. Convidamos você a refletir sobre seu desempenho até aqui e responder às questões propostas abaixo, escolhendo uma das seguintes opções:

> Sim.

> Preciso me preparar mais.

Questões

- Você reúne argumentos suficientes para expor e defender, de maneira clara e coerente, sua opinião em relação ao excesso de consumo na atualidade e seus efeitos?
- Você está apto a ler e compreender diferentes anúncios publicitários e reconhecer as características principais inerentes ao gênero?
- Você reúne conhecimentos linguístico-discursivos para produzir um anúncio publicitário em inglês?
- Você está preparado para escutar letras de música em inglês que abordam a relação entre a sociedade e o consumismo e compreender a mensagem expressa?
- Você se julga apto a analisar informações específicas em infográficos e compará-las a outras informações?

Refletindo sobre suas respostas

- Como você analisa a evolução do seu aprendizado em relação à unidade anterior?
- De que forma suas práticas de aprendizagem no decorrer desta unidade influenciaram suas respostas?
- O que você pode fazer para aprimorar ainda mais os conhecimentos adquiridos nesta unidade?
    a. Buscar por mais informações sobre o comportamento das pessoas em relação ao consumo, bem como sobre os efeitos do excesso de consumo na atualidade.
    b. Ler mais anúncios publicitários e observar as estruturas linguísticas e lexicais comumente usadas nesse gênero textual.
    c. Aprofundar meus conhecimentos em língua inglesa, usando recursos diversos, de forma que minha participação nas atividades seja mais ativa.
    d. Outros.

UNIT 8

HOW TECHY ARE YOU?

Chanpipat/Shutterstock.com

Nesta unidade você terá oportunidade de:

- refletir e discutir sobre a influência da tecnologia em nossas vidas;
- reconhecer os objetivos e algumas características de e-mails e escrever um;
- compreender um texto oral sobre a importância de escrever e-mails concisos;
- expor suas preferências sobre os meios de comunicação e discutir acerca de sua eficiência.

- O que podemos ver na imagem?
- Você acha que a tecnologia é uma ferramenta de mudança nas mãos das pessoas? Justifique.

STARTING OUT

 History / Computer Science

1. Below you will find a list of some top technological devices. Match them to their pictures.

- **a.** MP3 player
- **b.** GPS navigator
- **c.** Smartphone
- **d.** Digital camera
- **e.** Smart TV
- **f.** Kinect-based game

> Muitos termos de informática não foram traduzidos para a língua portuguesa, como por exemplo: *online*, *mouse*, *driver*, *spam*, *bluetooth* entre outros.

1.

2.
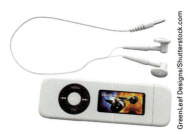

3.

4.

5.

6.

2. Choose the best alternatives to complete the sentences.

a. To connect with friends, people frequently use…

- text messages.
- social networks.
- online chats.
- e-mails.
- group discussion forums.
- Others: ♦

b. To connect with companies, people often use…

- letters.
- e-mails.
- social networks.
- tech support.
- FAQs.
- Others: ♦

> *FAQ* é um acrônimo da expressão *Frequently Asked Questions*, traduzida como "perguntas mais frequentes".

128 Unit 8 How Techy Are You?

READING COMPREHENSION

Before Reading

1. Look at the text below and answer: What text genre is this? How do you know that?

Reading

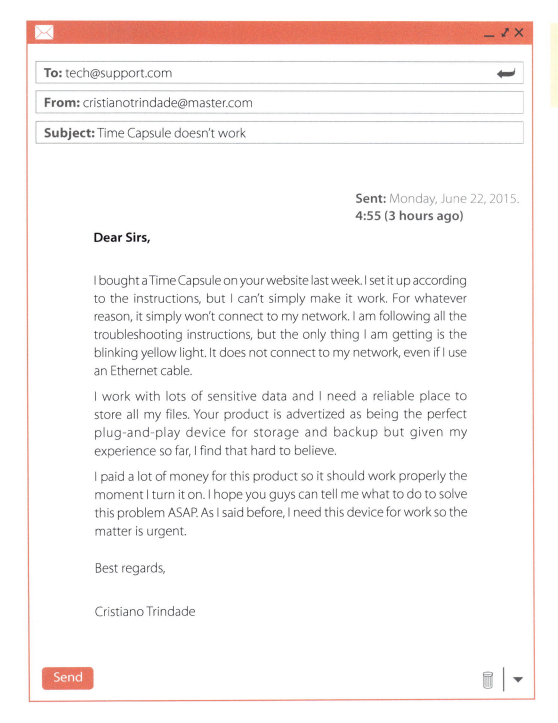

A abreviatura ASAP significa *as soon as possible* (o mais rápido possível) e é muito utilizada em e-mails.

2. Go back to the e-mail on page 129 and match the parts.

   a. Sender's e-mail address
   b. Sender's name
   c. Recipient's e-mail address
   d. Date of the e-mail
   e. Subject line

   - Cristiano Trindade
   - tech@support.com
   - cristianotrindade@master.com
   - Time Capsule doesn't work
   - Monday, June 22, 2015

   > O símbolo @ (arroba), usado em endereços eletrônicos para separar uma conta de e-mail da rede a qual ela pertence, é uma referência a *at* (em), portanto, usamos "at" quando falamos nosso endereço eletrônico. Para nos referirmos ao ponto, usamos "dot".

3. In your notebook, write T (True) or F (False). Then correct the false information.

   a. Cristiano Trindade had bought the Time Capsule weeks before it stopped working.
   b. Cristiano doesn't know what the problem with the Time Capsule is.
   c. He followed the instructions to correct the problem, but the only thing he got was a blinking yellow light.
   d. The product was on sale and very inexpensive. That's why Cristiano bought it.

4. Answer the questions below and then share your view with your classmates.

   a. Why do you think Cristiano preferred to send an e-mail rather than go to the store to complain?
   b. Which other solution would you consider if you were Cristiano? Justify.

5. Read the text below and then answer the questions.

   Netiquette: CC-ing and BCC-ing
   06/05/2014 by Chapman Upchurch

   CC-ing

   CC means Carbon Copy (who remembers those?). It sends a copy of your e-mail to those listed in the CC field.

   This is generally used when another person needs to be aware of the e-mail conversation but isn't directly involved.

   For example, you may be promising a client that a colleague will do something for them and it's courtesy for that colleague to be made aware of it.

   The dangers of CC-ing: Don't go overboard on CC-ing. The original recipient may find it rude, or the person who is copied in may find it irrelevant and annoying.

> **BCC-ing**
>
> BCC means Blind Carbon Copy and sends a hidden copy to those listed in the BCC field.
>
> This is generally used when a person needs to be aware of the e-mail conversation but you don't want their details to be made public.
>
> For example, you may be defusing a difficult situation with a client and need a superior to know your response, but you don't want the client to have your superior's e-mail address.
>
> The Dangers of BCC-ing: If the person who is BCC'd hits Reply All, the original recipient will see that they have been included.

Adapted from <www.cuaccountants.co.nz/blog/netiquette-ccing-and-bccing>. Accessed on November 13, 2015.

a. How are BCC and CC represented in e-mails in Portuguese?

b. In which circumstances is the use of BCC and CC is appropriate? Give some examples.

6. Read an extract from a guide about writing effective e-mails. Then read Cristiano's e-mail. Answer the questions below.

> [...]
>
> **Basic e-mail structure**
>
> Your e-mail message should be structured as follows:
>
> **Greeting**
>
> Body of the e-mail
> • Introduction - briefly explain the reason for the message (one sentence)
> • Main point - what is your purpose, explain what action is required by the recipient (one paragraph)
> • Supporting information - details, supporting information (one paragraph)
> • Next steps - explain what, if anything, happens next (one paragraph)
> • Conclusion - one closing sentence
> Salutation
> Signature
> [...]

Adapted from <www.icts.uct.ac.za/modules.php?name=News&file=article&sid=7093>. Accessed on November 14, 2015.

- Did Cristiano write an effective e-mail? How did you come to this conclusion?

After Reading

- How does technology impact on the way you interact with your friends and family?
- What do you think was considered high tech when your parents or family members were your age? Would you like to have lived at that time? Why/Why not?

VOCABULARY STUDY

1. Refer back to the e-mail on page 129 and look for words to complete, in your notebook, the excerpts of the texts below. The first letter is given to help you out.

   TIP
   O contexto vai ajudá-lo a compreender o significado das expressões; portanto, leia as frases inteiras antes de escolher as respostas adequadas e, sempre que possível, retorne ao texto para reler os trechos onde tais expressões aparecem.

   a. [...]
   Conquer the high seas or your local fishing spot with our marine line-up. From streamlined, highly-effective fishfinders to an entire p♦ marine network with sonar, radar and XM weather, we can outfit your rig. Some products are US versions. You may be leaded to Garmin US website. [...]

   Extracted from <www.garmin.co.in/softwareupdate/>. Accessed on November 11, 2015.

   b. [...]
   Information about t♦ your phone to check for malfunctions, and what you need to do to get it fixed. [...]

   Extracted from <www.nttdocomo.co.jp/english/support/trouble/>. Accessed on November 11, 2015.

   c. [...]
   S♦ d♦ encompasses a wide range of information and can include: your ethnic or racial origin; political opinion; religious or other similar beliefs; memberships; physical or mental health details; personal life; or criminal or civil offences. These examples of information are protected by your civil rights. [...]

   Extracted from <web.mit.edu/infoprotect/docs/protectingdata.pdf>. Accessed on June 24, 2015.

2. Pay attention to the phrasal verbs in bold in the extracts below. What do they mean?

   a. "I **set** it **up** according to the instructions, but I can't simply make it work."

   - discard, reject
   - install, prepare

   b. "I paid a lot of money for this product so it should work properly the moment I **turn** it **on**."

   - begin the operation
   - diminish the speed

3. The phrasal verbs below also refer to technological actions. Match them to their meanings.

   a. back up
   b. log off
   c. boot up
   d. print out
   e. pop up
   f. go down

   - make a copy of a document from a printer
   - make a second copy of a file or program
   - follow the procedures to finish using the computer
   - start by loading and initializing the operating system
   - fail to have Internet service
   - appear suddenly

Unit 8 How Techy Are You?

LANGUAGE IN CONTEXT

Present Continuous

1. Read this extract from the e-mail on page 129. Then identify the correct alternatives.

   "I **am following** all the troubleshooting instructions but the only thing I **am getting** is the blinking yellow light."

   a. The verb forms in bold are in the Present Continuous. They refer to…

   - actions that will happen in the future.
   - actions that are happening now.

   b. The structure of the Present Continuous is…

   - verb to be (*am*, *are* or *is*) + main verb in the *-ing* form.
   - verb to be (*am*, *are* or *is*) + main verb in the base form.

2. Read the text and find the Present Continuous verb forms. Then match questions and answers.

   > **15 Ways Technology Is Reinventing Society**
   > Megan Rose Dickey APR 28, 2013, 12:34 PM
   > Technology has the potential to radically change the way we live, and even how we relate to each other as human beings.
   > Technologies like 3D printing are changing manufacturing and democratizing creativity. Mobile apps are changing our buying behavior, with mobile commerce making up 20% of all e-commerce activity.
   > Nano-filtration is even changing the way we drink water.
   > At the same time, technologies like Google Glass are bringing the Internet closer to us than it ever has been before.
   > [...]

   Extracted from <www.businessinsider.com/15-ways-tech-is-reinventing-society-2013-4?op=1>. Accessed on June 24, 2015.

   a. Are 3D printing technologies **making** creativity more democratic?

   b. Is society **reinventing** technology?

   c. Is our buying behavior **changing** too?

   - No, that isn't happening. The opposite is happening.
   - Yes, we are modifying our shopping habits as well.
   - Yes, they are.

How Techy Are You? **Unit 8** 133

3. Go back to the previous activities and pay attention to the verb forms again. Then infer the rules for the Present Continuous.

   a. We often use the Present Continuous to talk about actions that are happening at or around the ♦ of speaking.

   b. In ♦ sentences, we use the subject followed by the verb to be and then the main verb in the ♦ form.

   c. In interrogative sentences, we invert the verb to be and the ♦. In negatives, we use ♦ between the verb to be and the main verb in the -ing form.

   d. Yes/No, + subject + ♦ is the pattern we follow for short answers.

   Refer to Language Reference pages 180 and 181 to learn more about the Present Continuous.

4. Use the verbs from the box in the Present Continuous to complete the text.

> leak   overheat   run   run out of

Why ♦ my Windows PC ♦ memory?

Jack Schofield
Thursday 11 June 2015

Judith's desktop computer runs slowly, and almost all its memory is being used even when she ♦ any applications. What might be going wrong?

[...]

Modern versions of Windows – the ones that followed Windows XP – are designed to use all your PC's physical memory: that's what it's there for. Either way, 3GB of memory plus a 4GB swapfile (a hidden file called pagefile.sys) is more than enough for the software you're running.

Windows could be running slowly because a program or device driver ♦ memory, because you don't have enough disk space, because a rogue process is running your processor at close to 100%, because your PC ♦, or because of a virus or other malware.

[...]

Extracted from <www.theguardian.com/technology/askjack/2015/jun/11/windows-pc-running-out-of-memory>.
Accessed on June 24, 2015.

Should

5. Read another extract from the e-mail on page 129 and answer the question in your notebook.

   "I paid a lot of money for this product so it **should** work properly the moment I turn it on."

   Does the modal verb *should* indicate a recommendation or a prohibition?

6. Complete part of the text *5 Reasons Technology Should Be Allowed in the Classroom*, with *should/should not* and the verbs *have, continue,* and *lose*. Then, in your notebook, answer the questions that follow.

[…]

Here are five reasons why educational institutions ♦ on that path instead of stepping back.

1. Students are technology natives. Using technology is second nature to students. They have grown up with it and incorporate it into almost every aspect of their lives. Notebooks, tablets and cellphones are all technology that students are accustomed to and can use as ancillary learning aids. They ♦ access to potential learning tools that have known benefits in a classroom.

2. Students use e-books. Many students are purchasing digital editions of textbooks instead of traditional printed copies for a variety of reasons, including cost efficiency, ease of accessibility, and environmental friendliness. E-books are typically accessed through a student's personal device, such as a notebook, tablet or cellphone. Students ♦ access to them to look up information during class.

[…]

Extracted from <www.edtechmagazine.com/higher/article/2014/11/5-reasons-technology-should-be-allowed-classroom>. Accessed on June 24, 2015.

What about you? How do you think technology should be used in the classroom? Justify your answer.

7. Unscramble the words to make a meaningful sentence to complete the cartoon caption. Write it down in your notebook.

turn off   date   cell phone   should   your   you   a   on

"♦... especially if it's smarter and cooler than you are."

Extracted from <www.glasbergen.com/wp-content/gallery/dating-amp-romance/toon762.gif>. Accessed on June 24, 2015.

WRAPPING UP

Tell a classmate about a technical problem you are having at the moment. He/She is going to give you a piece of advice using *should* or *shouldn't*. Use the prompts below as reference. Change roles. Then share your ideas with the class.

- printer / not print in color
- e-readers / not read the memory cards
- notebook / turn on and off by itself

LISTENING COMPREHENSION

Before Listening

1. Discuss the following questions with the whole group.
   - Who writes e-mails?
   - What kind of e-mails do people write?
   - What are e-mails written for?
   - What kind of e-mails can get effective results?
   - Do you believe e-mails are an effective means of communication? Explain.

Listening

2. You are going to listen to a certified life coach talking about how to write short and effective e-mails. Choose the correct answers to the questions.

   a. Dallas Travers does not introduce herself as a life coach. How does she do that?
      - She says she is a professional actress.
      - She says she is an advocate for actors.

   b. Has she ever had the experience of receiving a very long e-mail?
      - No, she hasn't.
      - Yes, she has.

   c. According to her, what is the first reaction people have when they get a long e-mail?
      - They immediately think they don't have time to read it.
      - They read it only if it's from a friend or a colleague.

   d. What happens to that e-mail then?
      - People reply to it as soon as possible.
      - People take a very long time to reply to it.

   e. How does Dallas feel when she receives a long e-mail from an actor or a student?
      - She feels it's hard for her to help someone who is not being clear.
      - She feels enthusiastic about helping them.

136   Unit 8   How Techy Are You?

16 **3.** Complete the transcript of the last part of the video recording with the expressions from the box. Then listen to Dallas Travers again and check your answers.

> hear back from someone
> get the feedback
> principle of simplicity
> too much work for them

> "So the ♦ and being concise is so important when it comes to your professional e-mails, and what I would like to do is share a few tips to help you be perceived as a professional, but also to help you ♦ you want from the e-mails that you are sending. Often times, if you don't ♦, it's probably because the e-mail you sent created ♦. So I'll give you a couple of tips. Then I'm actually going to give you a formula to follow when it comes to sending e-mails."

Transcribed from <www.youtube.com/watch?v=jBIG3_YVub0>. Accessed on June 24, 2015.

After Listening

- In your opinion, does Dallas show excitement when she talks? Justify.
- Do you feel like watching the video? Why?
- Which tips do you think she is giving people?

SPEAKING

Discuss the following questions in small groups.
✓ What are the means of communication you use on a daily basis?
✓ Do you think these are effective ways of communicating? Are there disadvantages in using them? Explain.
✓ Would you prefer to communicate in a different form? How? Why?

Share your experiences and thoughts with the whole group.

How different are your answers from your classmates'? Did you hear anything that made you change your mind about the use of any means of communication? What exactly?

WRITING

Write, send, and answer an e-mail. Follow the steps below.

Planning your e-mail

- Think of a subject for your e-mail. Here are some suggestions:
    - You bought a product over the Internet, but it hasn't been delivered yet.
    - You are a tourist and want some information from a Tourist Center.
    - You need to ask a teacher about school papers or tests.
    - You want to apply for a part-time job or send an application letter to a volunteering program etc.
- If you prefer, you can choose another topic.

Writing and rewriting your text

> **REFLECTING AND EVALUATING**
>
> Go back to your e-mail and make sure you paid attention to the following topics.
> - ✓ Is the subject line meaningful?
> - ✓ Is the text clear and concise?
> - ✓ Is the tone of your text appropriate?
> - ✓ Did you end your e-mail message with a closing sentence and the correct salutation?
> - ✓ Did you check your spelling and grammar?

- Write a draft of the e-mail in your notebook.
- Ask your teacher to read your e-mail.
- Make all the necessary adjustments.

After writing

- Send your e-mail to a classmate.
- Now imagine you are the recipient and answer it.
- How did the process of writing the e-mail help you understand this kind of communication?

SELF-ASSESSMENT

Chegamos ao fim da unidade 8. Convidamos você a refletir sobre seu desempenho até aqui e responder às questões propostas abaixo, escolhendo uma das seguintes opções:

Sim.   Preciso me preparar mais.

Questões

- Você tem conhecimento suficiente para expor sua opinião acerca da influência da tecnologia em nossas vidas?
- Você se sente capaz de ler e compreender diferentes *e-mails* em língua inglesa e reconhecer as características principais inerentes ao gênero?
- Você reúne conhecimentos linguístico-discursivos suficientes para redigir um *e-mail* em língua inglesa?
- Você está preparado para escutar e compreender textos orais acerca da importância de escrever *e-mails* concisos?
- Você se julga apto a expor suas preferências sobre os meios de comunicação e discutir acerca de sua eficiência?

Refletindo sobre suas respostas

- Como você analisa a evolução do seu aprendizado em relação à unidade anterior?
- De que forma suas práticas de aprendizagem no decorrer desta unidade influenciaram suas respostas?
- O que você pode fazer para aprimorar ainda mais os conhecimentos adquiridos nesta unidade?

    a. Buscar por mais informações sobre as vantagens e desvantagens do uso da tecnologia em nossas vidas.

    b. Procurar por diferentes modelos de *e-mails* em língua inglesa e identificar os elementos linguísticos e lexicais mais comumente usados.

    c. Aprofundar meus conhecimentos em língua inglesa, usando recursos diversos, de forma que minha participação nas atividades seja mais ativa.

    d. Outros.

Further Practice 4 – Units 7 & 8

1. Read the comic strips below and choose the appropriate answers to the questions.

Extracted from <www.amureprints.com/reprints/results?terms=consumerism&release_date_from=&release_date_to=&commit=Search>. Accessed on April 7, 2016.

Extracted from < www.amureprints.com/reprints/results?terms=consumerism&release_date_from=&release_date_to=&commit=Search>. Accessed on April 7, 2016.

   a. What do the comic strips have in common?
   - They are about inappropriate social behaviors.
   - The comic strips criticize consumerism.
   - They are about how modern technology can influence society.

   b. What are the correct verb forms needed to complete the first panel of the second comic strip?
   - pursuing / forsakes
   - pursue / forsake
   - pursuing / forsaking

2. Reflect on the comic strips and answer.
   Do you think buying things can make a person happy? Justify your answer.

3. Read the ad and discuss the questions.

Extracted from <www.adverbox.com/admin/wordpress/wp-content/uploads/2007/11/greenpeace4.jpg>. Accessed on November 11, 2015.

   a. Have you ever heard of Greenpeace? What do you know about it?

   b. Do you know why its work is important for the planet?

   c. What idea does the ad convey? Would you consider joining the organization? Why?

4. Identify the only alternative that we can't infer from the text.

   a. The sushi rolls in the ad represent the idea that we are victims of the trash we produce.

   b. The poster criticizes the food made with fish from polluted waters.

   c. The improper disposal of plastic bags leads to environmental contamination.

Extracted from <politicaladvertising.co.uk/2012/01/>. Accessed on July 01, 2015.

5. In your opinion, are polluted waters an effect of consumerism? Why/Why not?

Further Practice 4 – Units 7 & 8

6. Scan the fact sheet below and find out what the numbers refer to.

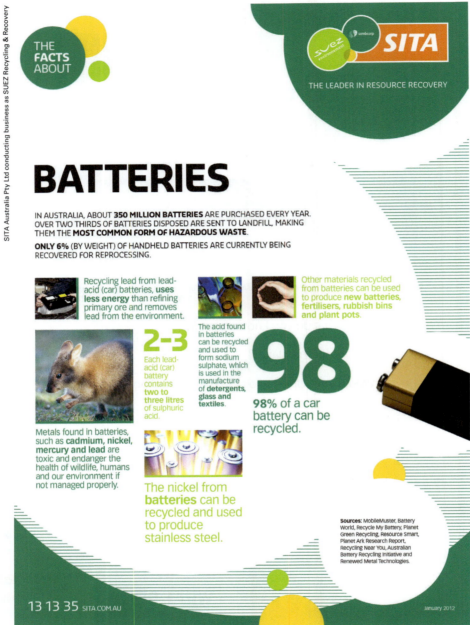

  a. 350 million. **b.** 98%. **c.** 2-3. **d.** 6%.

7. Answer T (True), F (False), or NM (Not Mentioned).

  a. The information on the fact sheet is true only in Australia.

  b. Cadmium is the most harmful metal to our environment.

  c. The acid found in batteries can be recycled.

  d. Batteries are the most hazardous kind of waste.

8. According to the fact sheet, what can be produced by using other materials recycled from batteries? Check.

a.

b.

c.

d.

e.

f.

9. How do you dispose of batteries? Is there an appropriate place in your community to throw them away? If so, share the information. If not, in your opinion, should that place be created? Why/Why not?

Units 7 & 8   Further Practice 3   143

Further Practice 4 – Units 7 & 8

10. Read part of an article from the *The Financial Post* and answer the questions.

> ### iPad Pro review: Apple Inc's 12.9-inch tablet is a slick, sophisticated beast.
> ### But you might not need it
>
> April Fong | November 11, 2015 | Last Updated: Nov 11 1:09 PM ET
>
> More from April Fong | @aprilfong
>
> I've had the iPad 2 for years now. It was great for surfing the Web, watching Netflix and writing emails at home and on-the-go — until I got a smartphone with a bigger screen.
>
> My tablet has been collecting dust and goes weeks without charging. I haven't felt an urge to buy a new one — and I'm not alone. According to market research firm IDC, global tablet shipments fell 12.6 per cent year-over-year in the third quarter, its fourth straight quarter of declines.
>
> But the iPad Pro may just help change that.
>
> Apple Inc. is hoping to make iPads interesting again with its new 12.9-inch tablet beast, which is designed with an optional Apple Pencil and snap-in Smart Keyboard. It's the Cupertino, Calif.-based company's most productive and sophisticated iPad yet — but that doesn't mean it's for everyone.
>
> [...]

Christoph Dernbach/DPA/AFP Photo

Extracted from <business.financialpost.com/fp-tech-desk/personal-tech/ipad-pro-review-apple-incs-12-9-inch-tablet-is-slick-sophisticated-beast-but-you-might-not-need-it>. Accessed on November 13, 2015.

a. Reread the passage "My tablet has been collecting dust and goes weeks without charging. I haven't felt an urge to buy a new one — and I'm not alone." Have you ever wanted something really hard and after you got it, you stopped using it? If so, why do you think this happened? If not, why do you think that happens?

b. In your opinion, what are the pros and cons of technology in communication?

EXAM PRACTICE

MUNIZ, Vik. *Pictures of Garbage.* 2008.

ABOUT VIK MUNIZ

Photographer and mixed-media artist Vik Muniz is best known for repurposing everyday materials for intricate and heavily layered recreations of canonical artworks. Muniz works in a range of media, from trash to peanut butter and jelly, the latter used to recreate Andy Warhol's famous *Double Mona Lisa* (1963) that was in turn an appropriation of Da Vinci's original. Layered appropriation is a consistent theme in Muniz's work: in 2008, he undertook a large-scale project in Brazil, photographing trash-pickers as figures from emblematic paintings, such as Jacques-Louis David's Neoclassical *Death of Marat*, and then recreating the photographs in large-scale arrangements of trash. The project was documented in the 2010 film *Waste Land* in an attempt to raise awareness for urban poverty. Muniz explained the work as a "step away from the realm of fine art," wanting instead to "change the lives of people with the same materials they deal with every day."

Extracted from <https://www.artsy.net/artist/vik-muniz>. Accessed on July 01, 2015

No que diz respeito às razões para adaptações e releituras de obras de arte já consagradas, podemos observar desde motivos econômicos; homenagem ao artista da obra original; desejo de contestar estéticas; ou até mesmo utilizá-las como ferramentas de crítica social ou cultural. Leia as proposições e escolha a alternativa correta a respeito da obra de Vik Muniz.

I. O artista Vik Muniz criou em sua adaptação de *A Morte de Marat* (Jacques-Louis David, 1793) um cenário fundamentado na crítica a uma modernidade cuja produção de lixo é gigantesca e tratada como algo efêmero e sem valor.

II. O artista brasileiro encontra eco em seu propósito ainda que a obra adaptada seja uma pintura e a adaptação, uma fotografia. As diferentes mídias contribuem para a produção de sentido da obra de Muniz.

III. Existem diferentes vozes na obra de Muniz que vão desde as vozes dos catadores de lixo, quem o produz até a voz do próprio lixo.

São verdadeiras:

a. Apenas a proposição I.

b. Nenhuma proposição.

c. As proposições II e II.

d. Todas as proposições.

e. Apenas a proposição III.

Career Planning

Unit 1

Social Worker

Social workers dedicate their careers to improving the quality of life of a group, individual, or community. They help many different types of clients, including elderly people who need care, children who need to be placed in foster homes, and the unemployed. They also help people apply for government benefits, and often play a critical role in domestic legal cases like child or spousal abuse.

There are two primary types of social care workers: direct-service social workers and clinical care social workers. Direct-service workers help their clients cope with problems that impact their everyday lives, while clinical care social workers provide mental health services to clients.

When a social worker starts working with a client, they use interviewing techniques to understand the client's situations, needs, and strengths. As they develop an understanding of the problem, they are able to begin creating a plan to improve their client's health or well-being.

Each situation requires a unique approach. Sometimes (as in abuse or neglect cases), social workers need to involve local law enforcement agencies to help solve a problem. Other times, they provide assistance by helping clients apply for benefits from government agencies, or referring them to organizations that provide resources like child care, healthcare, or food stamps.

[…]

How to Become a Social Worker

A minimum of a bachelor's degree is required for most social worker positions. Most employers prefer a bachelor's degree in social work, but some will also consider candidates who have a bachelor's in Psychology, Sociology, or a related field.

Bachelor's degree programs in social work directly prepare students for a career in the field. They include courses in community outreach, crisis intervention, community organizing, interviewing, assessments, and advocacy. Most programs also require students to complete an internship or supervised fieldwork before graduation. […]

Extracted from <resources.alljobopenings.com/social-worker-jobs>. Accessed on July 2, 2015.

1. What would you do in your community if you were a social worker? Justify your answer.

2. Would you like to work as a social worker? Why/Why not?

Unit 2

Sustainable Architect

Sustainable architects oversee the design and construction of buildings with a focus on the role a structure will play in its environment. For example, sustainable architects try to use only construction materials that won't contribute to landfills, as well as making certain all the building's systems and equipment have high energy-efficiency ratings. A sustainable architect's primary goal is to create attractive, affordable, and comfortable buildings that do not harm the environment, either during their construction or their lifetime.

[...]

Where to work

There are a number of places sustainable architects can find employment. They include:
- Architecture firms
- Colleges and universities
- Private consulting firms
- Product development and sales

Education & requirements

If you are a high school student considering a career as a sustainable architect, you should have strong marks or an interest in:
- Biology
- Mathematics
- Physics
- English
- Art
- Social Studies

In most cases, the minimum education requirement to work as a sustainable architect is a university graduate degree.
[...]

Extracted from <www.eco.ca/career-profiles/sustainable-architect>. Accessed on July 1, 2015.

1. Would you like to help the environment through your career choice just like a sustainable architect does? Justify your answer and give examples.

Career Planning

Unit 3

DJ

Disc Jockeys or DJs are required to play musical recordings in parties or events. Roles of these professionals vary depending on the purpose or the setting of the music. They may work for radio stations where they play musical selections from playlists. Among genres played by DJs are classic rock, heavy metal, adult contemporary, light rock, jazz, country western, gangsta rap, hip hop, among other music styles.

[...]

Skills

- Having interpersonal abilities.
- Being able to use sound boards and turntables.
- Having knowledge about musical trends.
- Being creative.
- Having good pronunciation.
- Being self-motivated and proactive.
- Having good communication skills.
- Having high attention to details.
- Being constantly informed about national news.
- Having good sense of humor.

Education

People who want to be **Disc Jockeys** or DJs do not need to meet a specific set of academic qualifications. Most employers just require a High School Diploma and sometimes a College degree. On-the-job experience is one of the most valuable points in this industry, so working at a College radio station is a great way to obtain suitable experience.

[...]

Extracted from <www.jobisjob.com/dj/job-description>. Accessed on July 1, 2015

1. Besides the skills mentioned in the text, what other skills do you consider necessary to become a DJ? Do you think you are suitable for this job? If not, would you like to be? Why?

Unit 4

Theater Actor

Successful theater actors are able to entertain, convey characters and express emotions in front of a live audience. Read on to learn about the training, skills, salary and job outlook for this sometimes stressful career.

Career Definition of a Theater Actor

A theater actor performs in plays and other types of live productions, such as skits, dinner theater and cabaret shows. Sometimes, they go on tour. Actors have a talent for performing and entertaining others. With the most common venue being a live stage, theater acting does not include the benefits of multiple takes and editing that film and television actors enjoy.

[…]

Required Education

Though a Bachelor of Arts in Theater is not necessary for becoming an actor or actress, formal training and education often help in this challenging and competitive industry. Earning a B.A. in Theater provides the opportunity for aspiring actors to learn acting skills in a structured environment and to practice their creative dramatic expression in front of live audiences. Providing more than just acting classes, a 4-year bachelor's degree in theater includes courses in all major aspects of performance and production, such as acting, directing, theater history, play writing, production design, costume design, makeup and theater technology.

Skills Required

Natural talent, persistence in pursuing auditions and luck are prominent factors in the success of a career in theater acting. The ability to memorize scripts and improvise under pressure are also helpful for aspiring actors.
[…]

Igor Bulgarin/Shutterstock.com

Extracted from <study.com/articles/Theater_Acting_Job_Description_and_Information_About_Starting_a_Career_in_Theater_Acting.html>. Accessed on July 1, 2015.

1. What do you know about the job market for actors and actresses in Brazil? In your opinion, which Brazilian cities offer the best opportunities? Why?

2. Is there anything in the acting career that attracts you? Explain.

Career Planning

Career Planning

Unit 5

Nutritionist

Nutritionists help to advance an understanding of how diet affects the health and well being of people and animals.

What does a nutritionist do?

Nutritionists generally work in a preventative role on a one-to-one and a group basis with patients of all ages. Unlike dieticians who primarily work with people who are ill, nutritionists mostly work with people who are healthy. Key responsibilities of the job include:

- researching how the body's functions are affected by nutrient supply
- investigating the relationship between genes and nutrients
- studying how diet affects metabolism
- examining the process of nourishment and the association between diet, disease and health
- providing health advice and promoting healthy eating
- advising about special diets
- educating health professionals and the public about nutrition
- working as part of a multi-disciplinary team/supporting the work of other health care professionals

[...]

Qualifications and training required

To become a nutritionist it is necessary to gain a degree in nutritional science, dietetics, or food science; or alternatively a life sciences degree that incorporates human physiology and biochemistry.

A postgraduate qualification in nutrition can be helpful and is essential for candidates without a suitable first degree in nutrition or dietetics. Employers may also require specific science A levels. Relevant work experience can be advantageous and can provide a useful insight into the profession.

[...]

Extracted from <targetjobs.co.uk/careers-advice/job-descriptions/276233-nutritionist-job-description>. Accessed on July 1, 2015.

1. Taking into consideration what you have read about this profession and what you know about it, do you agree that nutritionists are also health educators? Explain.

2. Do you think nutritionists can contribute to improving eating habits in your community? Justify and give examples.

Unit 6

Physical Education Teacher

by Michael Firth, Demand Media

Physical Education teachers are important figures in helping young people lead healthy lifestyles. P.E. teachers play an increasingly important role in the face of the staggering youth obesity crisis and the overall poor health of American society. Their passion for sport, physical activity and healthy living should motivate, inspire and educate students as to the benefits of these practices, which include joy and social interaction for the participants.

Duties

Physical education (P.E.) teachers plan, organize and deliver lessons consistent with the physical education curriculum of their students' grade level. This includes organizing skill development and game sessions for youth from kindergarten through high school. There is a focus on participation, cooperation and skill acquisition that furthers motor and cognitive as well as physical skills. Leadership and communication skills are also characteristic of a good physical education teacher. They often must demonstrate skills so remaining in shape and modeling good health is also critical.

Credentials

As teachers, they are required to have a degree or earn equivalency through training and experience. Certification is obtained by completing this credential and paying union and certification dues. They may be licensed by either the grade levels or subjects they teach including physical education. Master's degrees can be earned in the field of sports studies or a related instructional field. This credential typically enables teachers to earn more by qualifying for a higher pay rate.

[...]

PE Teacher Job Descriptions. Michael Firth, Demand Media
© 2013 Demand Media, Inc. U.S.A. All rights reserved.

1. In Brazil, there are some campaigns such as *Move Brasil* to encourage people to exercise. They offer different sport programs planned by Physical Education teachers. How can these programs contribute to improving exercise habits in your community? Would you like to be a PE teacher and work in campaigns like that? Why/Why not?

Career Planning   151

Career Planning

Unit 7

So what does a market analyst do, exactly?

Sinead Hasson
Tuesday, December 18 2012, 09:30 GMT

A career in analysis can be one of the most dynamic jobs in marketing. **Sinead Hasson** looks at what the job involves and the skills you'll need to succeed.

Chances are, when scrolling through job adverts, you skip right past market analyst roles to something which sounds more familiar or fun. But a career as an analyst can be one of the more dynamic positions in the marketing mix.

As a market analyst your job is to study information to help your employer or client make informed decisions about their market. This could range from what markets to launch a product in, to the price you might charge for something.

The information you analyse could be presented as numbers or words. For the former you need to be highly numerical and able to make sense of large sets of numbers. Statistical skills are useful – maths and analytics qualifications are also key. To analyse text, it's about digesting large quantities of information to understand what's relevant and what's not.

[...]

To get into market analysis you need to be able to show a particular set of skills on your CV. This may include knowledge of software such as Excel or SPSS, as well as broader statistical skills. Typical degree subjects are maths, social sciences, history and English, as these demonstrate the ability to analyse and interpret information. At interview you will be asked to illustrate your analytical skills. Think about your dissertation or major projects you have worked on – you will most likely have used analysis skills in your work for them.

[...]

Extracted from <www.theguardian.com/careers/why-consider-career-in-market-analysis>. Accessed on July 1, 2015.

1. How can a market analyst improve the economy of a community? Justify your answer.

2. Do you have any of the skills needed to get into market analysis? Would you like to get into it? Why?

Unit 8

Computer games tester

If you love computer games and enjoy working through things in a methodical way, this could be a great job for you. Games testing is a popular way of starting out in the games industry. It can be a good way to find out about the business as a whole. As a computer games tester it would be your job to play games many times to spot any bugs and mistakes that need to be fixed before the game goes on sale.

You don't need formal qualifications to become a tester. Your playing skills and knowledge of the games market will be more important to employers.

A good games tester has the ability to work under pressure and meet deadlines. You will also need patience, persistence and good office computer skills.

The work

Testing is a vital part of producing a computer game. As well as finding and recording programming faults (bugs), you would also play the role of the game's first public user. You would report on its playability and recommend improvements.

As part of a team of quality assurance (QA) testers, you would:

- play games in detail and in as many ways as possible
- test different levels and versions of a game
- check its performance against what the designer intended
- compare the game against others on the market
- note problems and suggest improvements
- try to work out what is causing a problem
- try to recreate the problem, recording the steps you took
- check accessibility options
- check for spelling mistakes and copyright issues such as logos
- check the text on packaging and in instruction manuals
- enter each 'bug report' into a quality management system
- work to strict deadlines

You would work closely with programmers, artists and designers before a game is released, and with customer support teams after it is on the market. Some jobs may involve checking and translating in-game instructions and manuals for overseas markets. […]

Adapted from <nationalcareersservice.direct.gov.uk/advice/planning/jobprofiles/Pages/computergamestester.aspx>. Accessed on July 1, 2015.

1. The job may sound easy, but a lot of the game success relies on the tester's opinion. Do you think you have the skills to play a game and report its pros and cons to your employer? Justify your answer.

2. In your opinion, what is the most appealing aspect of this career? Why?

Learning from Experience 1

Registre as respostas no caderno.

A Sustainability Summit and Exposition

Objectives

- use experience as the primary foundation for learning;
- learn about sustainability and think about sustainable actions;
- organize and conduct the event A Sustainability Summit and Exposition;
- make an online call for participation to invite participants and create posters to announce the event;
- reflect on the event considering the process and the final results.

Stage 1: Warming Up

> "If you think you are too small to make a difference, try sleeping with a mosquito." (Dalai Lama XIV)

Extracted from <www.goodreads.com/quotes/7777-if-you-think-you-are-too-small-to-make-a>. Accessed on June 20, 2015.

How can a single person help change the world into a more sustainable place? Discuss your opinion with your classmates.

Stage 2: Expanding Your Knowledge

Read the text below and find the actions that match your daily habits. Then compare your answers to your classmates.

Sustainability

Sustainability is based on the principle that everything we need for our survival, well-being and prosperity depends either directly or indirectly on the natural environment. It is the capacity for humans and nature to endure and prosper both short- and long-term by building, living, designing, planning and thinking in harmony with nature to ensure a stable, resourceful and prosperous future environmentally, economically and socially. Sustainability, which has been called a "Matter of life and death for people on the planet" by Julia Marton-Lefèvre, Director General, IUCN, is just as much about the economy, personal savings and health, and social equity, ethics and responsibility as it is the environment. Coming in many forms and fashions both large and small, sustainable actions immediately and especially overtime, bring great benefits to people and the planet. Incrementally, our everyday actions might be, or at least appear to be, minor in the grand scheme of things, but combined they add up and connect to either propel us forward towards personal, social, economical and ecological prosperity or drag us backwards towards an inevitable scarcity and degradation of ecological services and functions. From conserving water, to recycling e-waste to shopping organic, you will find a wide variety of actions you may begin taking today or plan over the weekend, such as building a compost, creating a certified wildlife habitat or painting your roof white, which can save you money, help improve your health and certainly allow you to make a difference for wildlife, wild places, your community and the world as a whole. According to the IUCN, Securing the web of life, "A sustainable future cannot be achieved without conserving biological diversity – animal and plant species, their habitats and their genes – not only for nature itself, but also for all 7 billion people who depend on it. The latest IUCN Red List is a clarion call to world leaders gathering in Rio to secure the web of life on this planet".

Extracted from <www.everythingconnects.org/sustainability.html>. Accessed on June 20, 2015.

Stage 3: Getting Down to Action

- Work in groups of 4. Some of you will be involved with the participants, others with the lecturers, some will make the online call for participation and others will be in charge of the posters to promote the event. Some students may also act as ambassadors to welcome participants from the school community or the school neighborhood, illustrating the inclusive and open culture of this project.
- Design a logo for the event.
- Make an online call for participation addressing the school staff so they can submit their proposals of talks, workshops, panel discussions, interaction boards or expositions on the topic of the summit. If possible, invite the community professionals (such as environmentalists, geographers, geologists, biologists, doctors, journalists, local business owners) to take part in the event as well.
- After scheduling the activities for the summit, make posters to promote the event inside and outside school.
- Plan in advance how you will capture the summit's content. Try to use different formats such as pictures, audio, and video recordings.
- Organize at least one meeting with speakers and/or moderators to explain their roles and your expectations for their contribution to the summit.

Stage 4: Analyzing and Sharing the Results

- Analyze the summit's records. Prepare and carry out a class presentation, in English, on the contents of the event, either through a slide show, graphics or charts.

Stage 5: Reflecting and Evaluating

- Has the event engaged members of the community, school staff and students in promoting sustainability awareness and understanding that all of us matter in this process?
- What have you learned from this experience? How can you proceed the next time you have to carry out a similar project so as to improve the outcome?

EXTRA RESOURCES

<switchboard.nrdc.org/blogs/kbenfield/a_trip_to_sustainaville.html>
<www.sustainabilitysummit.us/Home.aspx>

Accessed on July 6, 2015.

Learning from Experience 2

Students in Concert

Objectives
- Use experience as the primary foundation for learning;
- do some research about different topics regarding the school subjects and compose lyrics of a song about them;
- organize and conduct the event Students in Concert;
- create an online invitation and posters to promote the event;
- reflect on the event considering the process and the results.

Stage 1: Warming Up

Research Has Proven that Access to a Quality Music Education:

- Engages students in the classroom and increases graduation rates
- Improves early cognitive development, math and reading skills
- Enhances learning in other core subjects
- Develops critical thinking and leadership skills
- Fosters self-esteem and the ability to work cooperatively in teams

[…]

Extracted from <www.vh1savethemusic.org/why-music/benefits-to-the-brain>. Accessed on June 29, 2015.

How does music affect your life? Discuss your answer with your classmates.

Stage 2: Expanding Your Knowledge

Read the text and answer the question that follows.

How Songs Augment the Learning Process

[…]

Music is an enjoyable way to provide the base of prior knowledge that is so critical to learning. After singing songs in Spanish, an English-speaking child will recognize words as he studies Spanish language and culture, increasing his ability and his interest.

Music can be used to provide an introduction to, and stimulate interest in, subjects across the curriculum. As one's base of prior knowledge grows, interest and learning become easier, and a positive cycle is established.

The use of music in the classroom is consistent with theories of multisensory learning. Cognitive psychologists have confirmed what educators have long known – that we have a variety of different, but mutually enhancing, avenues to learning. Music is one such avenue. […]

Extracted from <www.songsforteaching.com/rationale.htm>. Accessed on June 25, 2015.

Do you think that integrating music to the school *curriculum* can be an effective learning strategy? Why?

Now read another part of the text and discover why music boosts the learning process. Then share your opinions with the class.

[...]

Research suggests that the more senses we use, the deeper and broader the degree of learning. Teachers are encouraged to use auditory, visual, kinesthetic and tactile modes to supplement the learning experience. While music is obviously an auditory activity, the kinesthetic, visual, and tactile modalities can be activated via clapping, dancing, and instrument playing. [...]

Music can function as a mnemonic device to aid recall of information. Just as we might use the expression, "In fourteen hundred and ninety-two, Columbus sailed the ocean blue." to jog our memories, we can use song to augment our recollection of facts. [...]

Extracted from <www.songsforteaching.com/rationale.htm>. Accessed on November 15, 2015.

Stage 3: Getting Down to Action

- Work in groups. Decide on a topic of a subject area you want to work on. Do some research about the topic to gather information for your song. Make up the lyrics to fit the chosen song. Remember to use language that is appropriate to your target audience.
- After getting language feedback from your teacher, start making the arrangements for the *Students in Concert* festival. Don't forget that "practice makes perfect", so rehearse as much as you can for your performance to meet the best expectations.
- Make an online invitation for the event and publish it on the school website. You can create posters to promote the event and display them around the school too. If possible, invite not only students from other classes and school staff members, but also your parents, your friends, and people from your community.
- Plan in advance to video record the event.
- Organize at least one rehearsal where all the participants can be together.

Stage 4: Analyzing and Sharing the Results

- Analyze the event's video recordings. Prepare and carry out a class presentation, in English, on the contents of the event, either through a slide show, graphics or charts.

Stage 5: Reflecting and Evaluating

- What have you learned from this experience? In which ways has this project promoted learning for you?
- How can you proceed the next time you have to carry out a similar task so as to improve the outcome?

EXTRA RESOURCES

<www.huffingtonpost.com/nicholas-ferroni/music-in-the-classroom_b_2072777.html>

<www.youtube.com/watch?v=LCqBX5INVKU>

Accessed on July 6, 2015.

Learning from Experience 3

How Healthy are You?

Objectives
- Use experience as the primary foundation for learning;
- learn about healthy living and think about healthier actions;
- organize and conduct a field research about snacks;
- analyze, present, and discuss the research findings;
- reflect on the task considering the process and the results.

Stage 1: Warming Up

> "The mind has great influence over the body, and maladies often have their origin there." (Jean Baptiste Molière, French writer).

Extracted from <www.psychologytoday.com/blog/the-mindful-self-express/201305/the-best-quotes-healthy-living>. Accessed on June 25, 2015.

Do you believe one can only have a healthy body if his/her mind is healthy too? Explain your reasons to your classmates.

Stage 2: Expanding Your Knowledge
Read the infographic and find the items that describe habits you already have. Then share your answers with a classmate.

---

11 Basic Guidelines for General Health and Longevity

Leading a common sense, healthy lifestyle is your best bet to produce a healthy body and mind, and increase your longevity. The following guidelines form the basic tenets of optimal health and healthy weight—foundational strategies that will not change, regardless of what marvels modern science comes up with next.

1. Eat a healthy diet
2. Replace sweetened drinks (whether they're sweetened with artificial sweeteners, sugar, or HFCS) with plenty of pure, clean water
3. Avoid all genetically engineered foods. There are nine primary GE food crops, but their derivatives are in over 70 percent of supermarket foods, particularly processed foods.
   – Soy
   – Corn
   – Canola Oil
   – Cottonseed
   – Hawaiian papaya
   – Alfalfa
   – Sugar from sugar beets
   – Some varieties of zucchini
   – Crookneck squash
4. Optimize your gut flora with fermented foods

> **5** Consume healthy fats, like butter, eggs, avocados, coconut oil, olive oil, and nuts
> **6** Eat plenty of raw food
> **7** Exercise regularly
> **8** Get an appropriate amount of sunlight to optimize your vitamin D levels
> **9** Limit toxin exposure
> **10** Get plenty of sleep
> **11** Manage your stress
> […]

Extracted from <www.mercola.com/infographics/general-health-guidelines.htm>. Accessed on June 25, 2015.

Stage 3: Getting Down to Action

- Work in small groups. Ask people from the school community what they frequently have for snacks throughout the day. Remember to ask the question in Portuguese so you can interview members from the whole community, who may not be fluent in English.
- Don't forget to document your conversations. You can video or audio record them, as long as the participants agree to that. You can also take pictures or notes.
- Collect all the data the group has found and bring it to class.
- After listing the most common items people have for snacks, discuss them with your group, choose one product, and conduct a research on its label. Is it healthy? Take notes.

Stage 4: Analyzing and Sharing the Results

- Prepare a class presentation to reveal the findings of the research. Use graphics or charts for a more comprehensible analysis of the data collected for your presentation. Discuss whether those products are healthy or unhealthy.
- Consider posting the results on the school website and/or making posters and hanging them inside the school, where participants can have access to the research findings.
- If possible, invite a doctor, a nutritionist, a dietitian, or another specialist from this area of expertise to come to school. They could talk about the community health profile and also contribute with some tips on how to live healthier and happier.

Stage 5: Reflecting and Evaluating

- How can this field research help participants from the school community? Think about your habits at school. What kind of food do they provide in the cafeteria, for example? Do you attend Physical Education classes?
- What have you learned from this experience? How can you expand this field research to effectively guide the school community towards a healthier lifestyle?

EXTRA RESOURCES

<www.everydayhealth.com/lifestyle/healthy-living/>

<writing.colostate.edu/guides/guide.cfm?guideid=23>

<www.researchconnections.org/childcare/datamethods/fieldresearch.jsp#qualitative>

Accessed on July 6, 2015.

Learning from Experience 4

Say NO to Consumerism

Objectives

- use experience as the primary foundation for learning;
- learn about compulsive consumerism and think about what we can do to escape that culture;
- start an ad campaign against consumerism;
- create a campaign poster to promote awareness about consumerism;
- reflect on the campaign considering the process and the results.

Stage 1: Warming Up

Has shopping turned into a lifestyle? Why do people buy stuff they don't need instead of making memories? Talk to your classmates.

Stage 2: Expanding Your Knowledge

Read an extract from a blog post entitled *Embracing Minimalism: Collect Moments, Not Things* and talk to your classmates about how it is related to your answers to the questions in stage 1. Then report your conclusions to the class.

Embracing Minimalism: Collect Moments, Not Things

Julie Beloussow / April 6, 2014 / Life / 3 Comments

Each day we are bombarded by advertisements for things.

We are told we need this shampoo for our hair to really shine, this cream for our skin to never age another day, this smartphone to make us hip, this tablet to end all tablets, this brand of shoes and this luxury car to truly live a comfortable life. *This*, *this*, *this*.

Is *this* really what it's all about? Is this what we work so hard for?

We don't work to meet our basic needs any more. We work to maintain a high standard, consumption driven lifestyle. We work to store and service the things we already own, the things we think we need to be happy. We work to buy more things in order to obtain the momentary thrill we get from doing so. More often than not, we fool ourselves into thinking *we need* something rather than just *want it*.

[…]

I would argue that most of the stuff we accumulate isn't necessary, but rather purchased in pursuit of attaining happiness. That is what most products are really advertising after all, under all the labels, bells and whistles, they're hawking happiness. It is a fleeting high we experience when we buy something, and when it fades we look for the next *thing*.

[…]

Extracted from <www.thirdperception.com/embracing-minimalism-collect-moments-not-things>.
Accessed on June 29, 2015.

To sum up, our consumerism is excessive when we consume more than we actually need.

In pairs, think of 5 reasons to escape excessive consumerism and write them down in your notebook. Then share your ideas with your classmates.

Stage 3: Getting Down to Action

- Work in small groups.
- Define which aspect of consumerism you want to focus on (such as its environmental impact, consumerism and social status, consumerism as slavery supporter, etc.).
- Do some research on the topic you've chosen and start planning your ad campaign poster. Do not forget to consider your target audience.
- Use visual effects and decide on the tone of your message: it may be emotional, humorous, scaring, surprising, etc. As long as the goal of getting the audience's attention is achieved, your choice will be well made.
- Show the poster to your teacher and make the necessary adjustments after getting feedback.
- Hang your poster on a wall inside the school and observe people's reactions to it.

Stage 4: Analyzing and Sharing the Results

- Talk to people around the school about the posters. Evaluate if they responded to your message as you expected them to.
- Carry out a class discussion on how you addressed the target audience to convince them to take action and adopt a new view of consumerism.
- Present your conclusions on the effectiveness of your campaign.

Stage 5: Reflecting and Evaluating

- How were the participants inspired by your cause?
- Has your campaign poster provoked a call for action? Explain your answer.
- Is there anything that you would like to change on your poster if you could? If so, what is it? If not, why not?
- How can you keep encouraging people towards a more active participation against consumerism?

EXTRA RESOURCES

<www.youtube.com/watch?v=EUeMVt3stAo>

<www.youtube.com/watch?v=6d8U6diy6lM>

<www.youtube.com/watch?v=ikeptr2-y3k&feature=youtu.be>

Accessed on July 6, 2015.

Studying for Enem

O Exame Nacional do Ensino Médio (Enem) foi criado em 1998 com a finalidade de avaliar o desempenho do estudante ao fim da educação básica. A partir de 2009, o exame passou a ser utilizado em caráter de seleção de ingresso para muitas universidades públicas e particulares do país. As provas são elaboradas tendo como referência quatro áreas do conhecimento: Matemática e suas Tecnologias, Ciências da Natureza e suas Tecnologias, Ciências Humanas e suas Tecnologias, Linguagens, Códigos e suas Tecnologias que, dentre outras disciplinas, abrange Língua Portuguesa e Língua Estrangeira Moderna (LEM).

A capacidade de interpretação de textos ocupa grande parte da prova, pois visa a avaliar como o candidato lida com situações recorrentes do cotidiano. Saber interpretar textos é considerado uma competência que, se bem desenvolvida, será útil em todas as disciplinas e não apenas naquelas que fazem parte da matriz Linguagens, Códigos e suas Tecnologias.

Para fazer uma boa prova, é importante que você leia tudo com muita atenção, esteja sempre bem informado sobre eventos da atualidade, estabeleça relações entre diferentes textos e norteie suas respostas pelo senso ético e cidadão.

Enem 2010

THE DEATH OF THE PC

The days of paying for costly software upgrades are numbered. The PC will soon be obsolete. And *BusinessWeek* reports 70% of Americans are already using the technology that will replace it. Merrill Lynch calls it "a $160 billion tsunami." Computing giants including IBM, Yahoo!, and Amazon are racing to be the first to cash in on this PC-killing revolution.

Yet, two little-known companies have a huge head start. Get their names in a free report from The Motley Fool called, "The Two Words Bill Gates Doesn't Want You to Hear…"

Click here for instant access to this FREE report
BROUGHT TO YOU BY THE MOTLEY FOOL

Disponível em: http://www.fool.com. Acesso em: 21 jul. 2010.

Ao optar por ler a reportagem completa sobre o assunto anunciado, tem-se acesso a duas palavras que Bill Gates não quer que o leitor conheça e que se referem

a. aos responsáveis pela divulgação desta informação na internet.
b. às marcas mais importantes de microcomputadores do mercado.
c. aos nomes dos americanos que inventaram a suposta tecnologia.
d. aos *sites* da internet pelos quais o produto já pode ser conhecido.
e. às empresas que levam vantagem para serem suas concorrentes.

Enem 2010

Viva la Vida

I used to rule the world
Seas would rise when I gave the word
Now in the morning and I sleep alone
Sweep the streets I used to own

I used to roll the dice

Feel the fear in my enemy's eyes

Listen as the crowd would sing

"Now the old king is dead! Long live the king!"

One minute I held the key

Next the walls were closed on me

And I discovered that my castles stand

Upon pillars of salt and pillars of sand

[...]

MARTIN, C. Viva la vida, Coldplay. In: **Viva la vida or Death and all his friends**. Parlophone, 2008.

Letras de músicas abordam temas que, de certa forma, podem ser reforçados pela repetição de trechos ou palavras. O fragmento da canção *Viva la vida*, por exemplo, permite conhecer o relato de alguém que

a. costumava ter o mundo aos seus pés e, de repente, se viu sem nada.

b. almeja o título de rei e, por ele, tem enfrentado inúmeros inimigos.

c. causa pouco temor a seus inimigos, embora tenha muito poder.

d. limpava as ruas e, com seu esforço, tornou-se rei de seu povo.

e. tinha a chave para todos os castelos nos quais desejava morar.

Enem 2010

Disponível em: http://www.chris-alexander.co.uk/1191.
Acesso em: 28 jul. 2010 (adaptado).

Definidas pelos países membros da Organização das Nações Unidas e por organizações internacionais, as metas de desenvolvimento do milênio envolvem oito objetivos a serem alcançados até 2015. Apesar da diversidade cultural, esses objetivos, mostrados na imagem, são comuns ao mundo todo, sendo dois deles:

a. O combate à AIDS e a melhoria do ensino universitário.

b. A redução da mortalidade adulta e a criação de parcerias globais.

c. A promoção da igualdade de gêneros e a erradicação da pobreza.

d. A parceria global para o desenvolvimento e a valorização das crianças.

e. A garantia da sustentabilidade ambiental e o combate ao trabalho infantil.

Enem 2011

How's your mood?

For an interesting attempt to measure cause and effect try Mappiness, a project run by the London School of Economics, which offers a phone app that prompts you to record your mood and situation.

The Mappiness website says: "We're particularly interested in how people's happiness is affected by their local environment – air pollution, noise, green spaces, and so on – which the data from Mappiness will be absolutely great for investigating."

Will it work? With enough people, it might. But there are other problems. We've been using happiness and well-being interchangeably. Is that ok? The difference comes out in a sentiment like: "We were happier during the war." But was our well-being also greater then?

Disponível em: http://www.bbc.co.uk.
Acesso em: 27 jun. 2011 (adaptado).

Studying for Enem

O projeto *Mappiness*, idealizado pela *London School of Economics*, ocupa-se do tema relacionado

a. ao nível de felicidade das pessoas em tempos de guerra.
b. à dificuldade de medir o nível de felicidade das pessoas a partir de seu humor.
c. ao nível de felicidade das pessoas enquanto falam ao celular com seus familiares.
d. à relação entre o nível de felicidade das pessoas e o ambiente no qual se encontram.
e. à influência das imagens grafitadas pelas ruas no aumento do nível de felicidade das pessoas.

Enem 2012

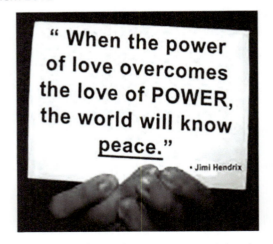

Aproveitando-se de seu *status* social e da possível influência sobre seus fãs, o famoso músico Jimi Hendrix associa, em seu texto, os termos *love*, *power* e *peace* para justificar sua opinião de que

a. a paz tem o poder de aumentar o amor entre os homens.
b. o amor pelo poder deve ser menor do que o poder do amor.
c. o poder deve ser compartilhado entre aqueles que se amam.
d. o amor pelo poder é capaz de desunir cada vez mais as pessoas.
e. a paz será alcançada quando a busca pelo poder deixar de existir.

Enem 2013

Steve Jobs: A Life Remembered 1955-2011

Readersdigest.ca takes a look back at Steve Jobs, and his contribution to our digital world.

CEO. Tech-Guru. Artist. There are few corporate figures as famous and well-regarded as former-Apple CEO Steve Jobs. His list of achievements is staggering, and his contribution to modern technology, digital media, and indeed the world as a whole, cannot be downplayed.

With his passing on October 5, 2011, readersdigest.ca looks back at some of his greatest achievements, and pays our respects to a digital pioneer who helped pave the way for a generation of technology, and possibilities, few could have imagined.

Disponível em: www.readersdigest.ca. Acesso em: 25 fev. 2012.

Informações sobre pessoas famosas são recorrentes na mídia, divulgadas de forma impressa ou virtualmente. Em relação a Steve Jobs, esse texto propõe

a. expor as maiores conquistas da sua empresa.
b. descrever suas criações na área da tecnologia.
c. enaltecer sua contribuição para o mundo digital.
d. lamentar sua ausência na criação de novas tecnologias.
e. discutir o impacto de seu trabalho para a geração digital.

Enem 2014

If You Can't Master English, Try Globish

PARIS – It happens all the time: during an airport delay the man to the left, a Korean perhaps, starts talking to the man opposite, who might be Colombian, and soon they are chatting away in what seems to be English. But the native English speaker sitting between them cannot understand a word.

They don't know it, but the Korean and the Colombian are speaking Globish, the latest addition to the 6,800 languages that are said to be spoken across the world. Not that its inventor, Jean-Paul Nerrière, considers it a proper language.

"It is not a language, it is a tool," he says.

"A language is the vehicle of a culture. Globish doesn't want to be that at all. It is a means of communication."

Nerrière doesn't see Globish in the same light as utopian efforts such as Kosmos, Volapuk, Novial or staunch Esperanto. Nor should it be confused with barbaric Algol (for Algorithmic language). It is a sort of English lite: a means of simplifying the language and giving it rules so it can be understood by all.

BLUME, M. Disponível em: www.nytimes.com.
Acesso em: 28 out. 2013 (fragmento).

Considerando as ideias apresentadas no texto, o *Globish* (*Global English*) é uma variedade da língua inglesa que

a. tem *status* de língua por refletir uma cultura global.
b. facilita o entendimento entre o falante nativo e o não nativo.
c. tem as mesmas características de projetos utópicos como o esperanto.
d. altera a estrutura do idioma para possibilitar a comunicação internacional.
e. apresenta padrões de fala idênticos aos da variedade usada pelos falantes nativos.

Language Reference

Unit 1

Imperative

Usamos o *Imperative* para dar instruções ou ordens, para fazer pedidos, dar sugestões ou conselhos.

Na forma afirmativa, construímos o modo imperativo usando o verbo no infinitivo sem a partícula *to*. Na forma negativa, colocamos *don't* antes do verbo.

Read the text carefully.

Don't discriminate any cultures.

Simple Present

O *Simple Present* é frequentemente usado para:

- falar de fatos ou opiniões

  A global citizen **contributes** to a better world.

- falar de hábitos ou rotinas

  Students **wear** uniforms in this school.

Na forma afirmativa, usamos o verbo no infinitivo sem a partícula *to* para as pessoas *I*, *you*, *we* e *they* e acrescentamos -s, -es ou -ies ao final do verbo para as terceiras pessoas *he*, *she* e *it*.

Regras de ortografia para acréscimo de -s, -es ou -ies ao fim dos verbos na terceira pessoa do singular do *Simple Present*:

- Para a maioria dos verbos, acrescentamos -s:

  enjoy – enjoy**s**

  love – love**s**

  want – want**s**

- Para verbos terminados em -o, -s, -ss, -ch, -sh, -x ou -z, acrescentamos -es:

  do – do**es**

  miss – miss**es**

  watch – watch**es**

- Para verbos terminados em -y antecedido por uma vogal, acrescentamos -s:

  annoy – annoy**s**

  play – play**s**

  buy – buy**s**

- Para verbos terminados em -y antecedido por uma consoante, trocamos o -y por -i e acrescentamos -es:

  classify – classif**ies**

  try – tr**ies**

  worry – worr**ies**

- O verbo *have* é uma exceção, pois é um verbo irregular. Nesse caso, usamos a forma *has* para *he*, *she* e *it*.

  have – **has**

Na forma negativa, usamos os verbos auxiliares *do not* (*don't*) e *does not* (*doesn't*) antes do verbo principal. *Don't* é usado para as pessoas *I*, *you*, *we* e *they* e *doesn't* é usado para as terceiras pessoas do singular *he*, *she* e *it*.

Na forma interrogativa, usamos os auxiliares *do* e *does* antes do sujeito e seguidos pelo verbo principal. *Do* é usado para as pessoas *I*, *you*, *we* e *they*, e *does* é usado para as terceiras pessoas do singular *he*, *she* e *it*.

Observe os exemplos no quadro a seguir.

Affirmative	Negative	Interrogative
I **work** downtown.	I **do not** (**don't**) work downtown.	**Do** I work downtown?
You **need** our help.	You **do not** (**don't**) need our help.	**Do** you need our help?
He **has** a beach house.	He **does not** (**doesn't**) have a beach house.	**Does** he have a beach house?
She **cries** at weddings.	She **does not** (**doesn't**) cry at weddings.	**Does** she cry at weddings?
It **costs** too much.	It **does not** (**doesn't**) cost too much.	**Does** it cost too much?
We **like** Chinese food.	We **do not** (**don't**) like Chinese food.	**Do** we like Chinese food?
You **exercise** in the morning.	You **do not** (**don't**) exercise in the morning.	**Do** you exercise in the morning?
They **speak** Spanish.	They **do not** (**don't**) speak Spanish.	**Do** they speak Spanish?

Short Answers

Para formarmos *short answers* (respostas curtas) com o *Simple Present*, usamos os verbos auxiliares *do* ou *does* para respostas afirmativas e *don't* ou *doesn't* para respostas negativas.

	Short answers	
	Affirmative	**Negative**
Do you have classes in the morning?	Yes, **I do**.	No, **I don't** (**do not**).
Does she usually arrive late?	Yes, she **does**.	No, she **doesn't** (**does not**).

1. Read the text and identify the verbs that express facts or indicate habits/routines and the verbs that give recommendations on what to do to become a global citizen. Then make a similar chart to the one below in your notebook and write the verbs in the appropriate column.

What is a global citizen?

[...]

We don't ask for charity, we ask for justice. And we put our hands up to write the next chapter in the greatest story yet to be told... the end of extreme poverty.

Using Global Citizen we unite and amplify our collective voice, working together to learn more and take action on issues that perpetuate extreme poverty. We share our passion for the issues we care about, and mobilise around crucial moments for change.

Help us build the movement of Global Citizens taking action for change. Get started by reading our manifesto, and seeing the latest stories and actions in our key themes of food and hunger, education, health, water and sanitation, enterprise and innovation, women and girls, and sustainability.

Extracted from <www.globalcitizen.org/en/content/what-is-a-global-citizen/>. Accessed on June 04, 2015.

Verbs that express facts or indicate habits/routines	Verbs that give recommendations on what to do
♦	♦

Language Reference 167

Language Reference

2. Based on the world issues presented below, write what can be done to resolve some of these issues. Use the sentences from the box. There is an example for you.

> End economic inequality, violence against women, and many other forms of gender discrimination.
> Ensure that poor farmers have the land and the resources they need.
> Promote global public goods and policy coherence for pro-poor health.
> Provide children, teachers, families and communities with the infrastructure, training, resources, services and support they need.

a. Well-fed people create stable communities, perform better in school and take advantage of the opportunities to end extreme poverty. The world has more than enough food to feed everyone, it's time to make sure everyone gets enough to thrive.

Extracted from <www.globalcitizen.org/en/issue/food-hunger/>. Accessed on June 04, 2015.

Ensure that poor farmers have the land and the resources they need.

b. The world has cut the number of children without an education in half. This progress must extend to the over 50 million still left out. Educated and healthy children will lead their communities out of poverty and build the thriving nations of tomorrow.

Extracted from <www.globalcitizen.org/en/issue/education/>. Accessed on June 04, 2015.

c. Healthy people are able to live fuller, happier lives. They are able to pull themselves out of extreme poverty. For pregnant mothers, newborns and children a healthy life requires vaccines and access to healthcare. Everyone must be healthy to end poverty.

Extracted from <www.globalcitizen.org/en/issue/health/>. Accessed on June 04, 2015.

d. Girls and women are essential to building healthier, better-educated and sustainable communities. Women and girls are too often afflicted with some of the harshest aspects of poverty. Instead of victims, women and girls can be powerful community leaders.

Extracted from <www.globalcitizen.org/en/issue/women-girls/>. Accessed on June 04, 2015.

Unit 2

Simple Future with Will

Usamos o auxiliar *will* para nos referirmos a diferentes situações no futuro, tais como:

- Fazer previsões:

    *The event **will be** a huge success.*

- Falar sobre decisões tomadas espontaneamente:

    *It's cold. **I'll put on** my jacket.*

- Fazer pedidos:

    ***Will** you **help** me with the beverages?*

- Fazer promessas:

    *I **won't leave** you alone.*

Na forma afirmativa, usamos *will* seguido do verbo principal no infinitivo.

Na forma negativa, acrescentamos *not* entre *will* e o verbo principal no infinitivo.

Na forma interrogativa, usamos *will* antes do sujeito.

Observe os exemplos no quadro a seguir.

Affirmative	Negative	Interrogative
I **will** / I'**ll meet** a friend for dinner tomorrow.	I **will not** / I **won't meet** a friend for dinner tomorrow.	**Will** I **meet** a friend for dinner tomorrow?
You **will** / You'**ll enjoy** the concert.	You **will not** / You **won't enjoy** the concert.	**Will** you **enjoy** the concert?
He **will** / He'**ll call** us after the meeting.	He **will not** / He **won't call** us after the meeting.	**Will** he **call** us after the meeting?
She **will** / She'**ll travel** on business.	She **will not** / She **won't travel** on business.	**Will** she **travel** on business?
It **will** / It'**ll rain** tonight.	It **will not** / It **won't rain** tonight.	**Will** it **rain** tonight?
We **will** / We'**ll attend** a conference.	We **will not** / We **won't attend** a conference.	**Will** we **attend** a conference?
You **will** / You'**ll become** famous.	You **will not** / You **won't become** famous.	**Will** you **become** famous?
They **will** / They'**ll walk** home after the game.	They **will not** / They **won't walk** home after the game.	**Will** they **walk** home after the game?

Short Answers

Para formarmos *short answers* (respostas curtas) no *Simple Future*, usamos o auxiliar *will* para respostas afirmativas e *won't* para respostas negativas.

	Short answers	
	Affirmative	Negative
Will he talk about environmental problems?	Yes, he **will**.	No, he **won't** (**will not**).
Will they buy a second-hand car?	Yes, they **will**.	No, they **won't** (**will not**).

1. Read the following text and pay attention to the highlighted verb forms. Then check the correct answer to this question: What do these verbs have in common?
   - They are used to talk about facts, opinions, and routines.
   - They are used to talk about future actions.

Language Reference 169

Language Reference

IB World Student Conferences

At each IB World Student Conference, students from around the world collaborate to develop innovative solutions to global issues.

Students hear from inspiring speakers, engaging in thoughtful inquiry focused on the conference theme, in small sessions. They also participate in excursions and recreational activities.

These experiences encourage the building of meaningful relationships with peers, and develop international understanding and leadership skills that benefit participants far beyond the conference week.

How do students benefit from the conference?

Each IBWSC has a theme with an activity and Global Action Team programme constructed around it. Speakers from around the world **will challenge** students with real, significant global issues. Working in Global Action Teams, students **will develop** creative ways to address the problems posed by conference leaders and propose solutions to these issues in the form of creativity, action, service (CAS) projects.

What do students take back to school?

Students who attend an IB World Student Conference return to their schools and communities with many new experiences to share. They not only develop leadership skills and meet other like-minded students, but also have the opportunity to interact with university faculty and world-renowned speakers representing a wide variety of disciplines and areas of expertise. These skills and experiences are designed to inspire students in the creation of action plans that are theme-based and can be implemented in their local communities.

Register for the next conference

For more information on the 2016 IB World Student Conferences, and to register, please visit our conferences section.

You can also read about previous IB World Student Conferences.

Extracted from <www.ibo.org/en/university-admission/ib-world-student-conference/>. Accessed on July 06, 2015.

2. Read the three first paragraphs of the text in activity 1 and identify the verbs in the Simple Present that are used to express facts, opinions, or routines.

Unit 3

Adjectives

Adjectives são palavras que qualificam substantivos. Eles geralmente são posicionados antes dos substantivos que qualificam:

*I will download **free** music to my MP3 player.*
*Does the **new** teacher have access to the **technological** material?*

Observe também que adjetivos não são flexionados em gênero ou número plural em inglês:
*I don't need all these **technological** devices.*

Também é comum vermos *adjectives* posicionados depois do verbo *to be*:
*Those tablets aren't **old**.*

Plural of Nouns

Como regra geral, para formarmos o plural dos substantivos, acrescentamos *s*:

*text – text**s***   *magazine – magazine**s***   *lamp – lamp**s***

Porém, existem algumas exceções. Observe:

- Para formar o plural dos substantivos terminados em *-ch*, *-sh*, *-s*, *-ss*, *-x*, *-z* e a maior parte dos substantivos terminados em *-o*, acrescentamos *es*:

    *watch – watch**es***   *gas – gas**es***   *crucifix – crucifix**es***   *potato – potato**es***
    *wish – wish**es***   *kiss – kiss**es***   *quiz – quizz**es***

Alguns substantivos terminados em *-o* fazem o plural seguindo a regra geral, com o acréscimo de *-s*, tais como: *stereos*, *photos*, *cellos*, *videos* etc.

- Nos substantivos que terminam em *-f* ou *-fe*, trocamos essas letras finais por *ves*:

    *knife – kni**ves***   *leaf – lea**ves***   *self – sel**ves***

Alguns substantivos terminados em *-f* ou *-fe* formam o plural com *-s*, tais como: *roofs* e *chiefs*.

- Nos substantivos que terminam em consoante + *-y*, trocamos o *-y* por *-i* e então acrescentamos *-es*:

    *gallery – galler**ies***   *possibility – possibilit**ies***   *story – stor**ies***

- Alguns substantivos têm formas irregulares de plural:

    *child – **children***   *foot – **feet***
    *woman – **women***   *man – **men***
    *mouse – **mice***   *person – **people***
    *tooth – **teeth***

- Alguns substantivos têm somente uma forma:

    clothes   *money*   *series*
    jeans   *scissors*   *shorts*

1. Unscramble the letters and form words to qualify the nouns below. Then complete the first part of the text *How has the Internet and Social Media Changed the Music Industry?* with the adjective-noun combinations.

    a. ♦ (w / n / e)   element
    b. ♦ (i / g / b)   time
    c. ♦ (e / e / i / t / d / n / f / r / f)   place
    d. ♦ (c / l / n / t / c / r / e / e / i / o)   copy
    e. ♦ (d / h / a / r)   copies
    f. ♦ (s / a / n / i / i / g / p / r)   artists
    g. ♦ (a / e / e / d / w / r / p / s / i / d)   problem

Language Reference

How has the Internet and Social Media Changed the Music Industry?
By Laura Harrison | July 23, 2014

The Internet has transformed the world and the music industry as we know it. Before everybody was hooked up to the World Wide Web, the music scene was a very ♦. Twenty years ago, consumers relied more heavily on CDs, The Charts and the radio. It was a time when mix tapes were rife and people brought CDs or *cassettes* to parties.

Advancements in technology meant that ♦ of music were no longer a necessity- the introduction of the digital mp3 pushed out the requirement to own CDs. Similar to mix tapes, listeners would borrow a friend's CD, copy the music to their computer and have an ♦ of the CD.

The Internet shook things up further, as connection speeds increased, file sharing became more common. Consumers illegally used programmes like Napster and Limewire to pirate music, waiting for many hours to download a single track. Pirated music became a ♦ for record labels as there was no way to police the music duplication.

The advent of social networking also brought a whole ♦ to the music industry, with MySpace providing a platform for users to follow musicians and discover new bands. YouTube has meant that consumers no longer have to rely on MTV or purchase a band's video or DVD to watch their music videos. Streaming services like Spotify and Pandora give listeners access to any music from anywhere with an Internet connection.

So technology and the Internet have changed the way we source and listen to music but it has also changed the way music is produced. Where twenty years ago, ♦ would rely on corporate bigwigs to listen to their demo disc, the Internet has put some power back in their artist's hands.

Thanks to the Internet, musicians and singers now have more control over their own fates. They are able to produce their own track, upload it to the Internet and promote it accordingly. This not only helps listeners discover them but also producers, helping them to get signed and make it ♦.

[...]

Adapted from <www.socialnomics.net/2014/07/23/how-has-the-internet-and-social-media-changed-the-music-industry/>. Accessed on July 03, 2015.

Unit 4

-Ing endings

As palavras terminadas com o sufixo *-ing* podem desempenhar as funções de:

- Substantivos

Interpreting a work of art is not an easy task.

- Verbos

They aren't coming home for lunch.

- Adjetivos

Which is the most interesting museum you have visited?

Superlative (long and short adjectives)

Os adjetivos também podem ser usados para comparar pessoas, lugares ou ações em um grupo ao qual pertencem, quando queremos dizer que tal elemento comparado pertence ao grau mais alto em um determinado aspecto.

Para formarmos o superlativo de adjetivos de uma sílaba e de alguns adjetivos de duas sílabas, acrescentamos a terminação -est ao final destes. Note que o artigo definido *the* é usado antes dos adjetivos no grau superlativo.

long – the long**est**

fast – the fast**est**

nice – the nic**est**

big – the bigg**est**

Estude as regras ortográficas para formar adjetivos no grau superlativo:

- Adjetivos terminados em -e são acrescidos de -st: *wise – the wis**est***
- Adjetivos terminados em consoante + vogal + consoante têm a última consoante dobrada: *fat – the fat**test***
- Adjetivos terminados em -y precedido por uma consoante perdem o *y* e são acrescidos de -iest: *busy – the bus**iest***

Para formarmos o superlativo da maioria dos adjetivos de duas sílabas e de adjetivos com três ou mais sílabas, usamos a estrutura *the most* antes deles.

famous – **the most** famous

beautiful – **the most** beautiful

interesting – **the most** interesting

tiring – **the most** tiring

Observe os exemplos a seguir:

*Geography is **the most interesting** school subject for me.*

*Anna is **the prettiest** girl in my family.*

*Which is **the most expensive** hotel downtown?*

*The teacher is going to choose **the tallest** students to join the basketball team.*

Note que há algumas formas irregulares de superlativos:

good – **the best**

bad – **the worst**

far – **the farthest / the furthest**

1. Read the gallery label texts and identify the word classes of the words in bold. Write N for nouns, V for verbs or A for adjectives next to each word.

a.

By **repurposing** methods of television, cinema, and video production, Ken Okiishi's work responds to the migration of images, information, and language in a world increasingly reshaped by digital media.

gesture/data combines video **recordings** with painting to create hybrid image-objects suspended between analog and digital technologies. The artist was inspired by viewing *Wood, Wind, No Tuba* (1980), an abstract painting by Joan Mitchell (American, 1925-1992), in MoMA's Agnes Gund Garden Lobby. As he photographed the **painting** with his iPhone, Okiishi was fascinated by the transformation of its original scale and physical presence into a small, portable field of **glowing** pixels and code. […]

Gallery label from *Cut to Swipe*, October 11, 2014-March 22, 2015

Adapted from <www.moma.org/collection/object.php?object_id=180678>. Accessed on July 06, 2015.

Language Reference

b.

Roysdon's work encompasses **art-making**, choreography, curating, **writing**, and **organizing**. *Sense and Sense* is part of her ongoing exploration of how political movements are represented, which hinges on a broad **understanding** of choreography as organized movement. Roysdon is interested in "the way an idea of 'free movement' and people demonstrating comes to be represented by an abstraction and in turn comes to represent the idea of the city." For this piece, she collaborated with the performance artist MPA, whose work examines the social and political implications of the body in space.

MPA lays on her side and mimics **walking**, her body pressed to the ground, through Stockholm's **buzzing** central square, Sergels Torg, a historical site of countless political demonstrations. [...]

Gallery label from *Sites of Reason: A Selection of Recent Acquisitions*, June 11-September 28, 2014

Extracted from <www.moma.org/collection//browse_results.php?object_id=179338>. Accessed on July 06, 2015.

Unit 5

Wh- Question Words

Usamos pronomes interrogativos (*wh- question words* ou *wh- words*) para fazermos perguntas. Tais perguntas são chamadas *wh- questions*.

Veja algumas *wh- question words* mais frequentes no quadro a seguir.

Pronomes interrogativos (wh- question words / wh-words)	Usados quando queremos saber sobre	Exemplos
What	ação, coisa	**A:** *What will you do tonight?* **B:** *I'll go to the movies.*
When	tempo	**A:** *When will the class finish?* **B:** *At 1 p.m.*
Where	lugar	**A:** *Where is my cell phone?* **B:** *It's under the book.*
Which	elemento específico	**A:** *Which dress do you want, the short or the long one?* **B:** *I want the long one.*
Who	pessoa	**A:** *Who is she?* **B:** *She's my sister Rose.*
Whose	posse	**A:** *Whose card is this?* **B:** *It's Ryan's.*
Why	razão	**A:** *Why do you look so sad?* **B:** *Because I'm sick.*
How	modo ou maneira	**A:** *How are you?* **B:** *I'm fine, thanks.*
How big	tamanho	**A:** *How big is your house?* **B:** *It's not very big.*
How many	quantidade	**A:** *How many flash drives do you have?* **B:** *I have only one.*

Pronomes interrogativos (wh- question words / wh-words)	Usados quando queremos saber sobre	Exemplos
How much	quantidade ou preço	**A:** How much juice do you want? **B:** Just a little, please. **A:** How much is that tablet? **B:** It's very expensive.
How often	frequência	**A:** How often does your sister eat out? **B:** Never. She always eats at home. She loves to cook.
How old	idade	**A:** How old are they? **B:** They're 16.

1. Complete the quiz with the *wh-* questions words: *how often, what, how much* and *which*. In pairs answer the six questions. Then check the correct answers with your teacher.

Quiz: Healthy eating

Question 1
♦ _____ should you eat fish, according to experts?
- A: Once a week
- B: Twice a week
- C: Every day

Question 2
♦ _____ contains the most vitamin C?
- A: Milk
- B: Sprouts
- C: Oranges

Question 3
♦ _____ water do experts reckon people should drink every day?
- A: 1 litre
- B: 2 litres
- C: 3 litres

Question 4
♦ _____ calcium do our bodies need to be healthy?
- A: 100 mg per day
- B: 400 mg per day
- C: 700 mg per day

Question 5
♦ _____ fat is the worst type for our health?
- A: Polyunsaturated fat
- B: Saturated fat
- C: Monounsaturated fat

Question 6
♦ _____ percentage of our daily calorie intake (energy) should come from carbohydrates?
- A: 50 per cent
- B: 80 per cent
- C: 100 per cent

Extracted from <news.bbc.co.uk/cbbcnews/hi/newsid_2640000/newsid_2646600/2646621.stm>. Accessed on July 03, 2015.

Language Reference

Unit 6

Simple Past

O *Simple Past* é usado para falarmos de ações e situações que ocorreram em um tempo definido no passado.

Para formarmos o *Simple Past* dos verbos regulares, acrescentamos as terminações *-ed*, *-d* ou *-ied* ao final. Já os verbos irregulares têm sua forma própria no *Simple Past*.

Allan **visited** us last week.
We **went out** with our friends yesterday evening.

Na forma negativa, inserimos *not* entre o auxiliar *did* e o verbo principal.
Allan **did not** (didn't) **visit** us last week.
We **did not** (didn't) **go out** with our friends yesterday evening.

Na forma interrogativa, invertemos a posição do verbo auxiliar *did* e do sujeito.
Did Allan **visit** us last week?
Did we **go out** with our friends yesterday evening?

Observe os exemplos na tabela abaixo.

Affirmative	Negative	Interrogative
I **watched** a movie on TV last night.	I **did not** / I **didn't watch** a movie on TV last night.	**Did** I **watch** a movie on TV last night?
You **sent** the e-mail to Susan.	You **did not** / You **didn't send** the e-mail to Susan.	**Did** you **send** the e-mail to Susan?
He **bought** me a ring.	He **did not** / He **didn't buy** me a ring.	**Did** he **buy** me a ring?
She **studied** all night long.	She **did not** / She **didn't study** all night long.	**Did** she **study** all night long?
It **rained** a lot yesterday morning.	It **did not** / It **didn't rain** a lot yesterday morning.	**Did** it **rain** a lot yesterday morning?
We **slept** late.	We **did not** / We **didn't sleep** late.	**Did** we **sleep** late?
You **ate** too much cake.	You **did not** / You **didn't eat** too much cake.	**Did** you **eat** too much cake?
They **called** us two weeks ago.	They **did not** / They **didn't call** us two weeks ago.	**Did** they **call** us two weeks ago?

Short Answers

Para formarmos as respostas curtas (*short answers*) no *Simple Past*, usamos o auxiliar *did* para respostas afirmativas e *didn't* para respostas negativas.

	Short Answers	
	Affirmative	Negative
Did she make a mistake?	Yes, she **did**.	No, she **didn't** (**did not**).
Did they grow up in the suburbs?	Yes, they **did**.	No, they **didn't** (**did not**).

Note que no *Simple Past* frequentemente especificamos quando as ações aconteceram, por isso é comum usarmos expressões de tempo, como: *yesterday, last, ago* etc.

1. Read the text and identify the verbs in the Simple Past tense. Then, in your notebook, make a chart similar to the one on the following page and complete it accordingly.

More about Michael Phelps

Diagnosed with Attention Deficit disorder, Phelps was directed towards swimming in 1992 at the age of just seven in order to provide him with an outlet for his unbounded energy. After that, his transformation into an unbeatable swimmer appeared inexorable, and he broke record after record as he rose through the age categories.

The Baltimore Bullet's first Olympic appearance came in 2000 in Sydney when he was chosen for the US swim team at the age of just 15 – the youngest American swimmer selected for the Olympic Games in almost 70 years.

He failed to win a medal in Australia but it was clear that Sydney was just a learning experience and this was to prove no setback. A year later Phelps became the youngest male swimmer to break a world record with a win in the 400m freestyle at the 2001 World Aquatics Championship – a taste of future glory.

The next two years saw Phelps amass a haul of gold and silver medals at international swim meets and break numerous world records in the 200m and 400m individual medley races. His tally at the 2003 World Aquatic Championship of four golds and two silvers, along with five world records, set the scene for a thrilling performance at the 2004 Olympic Games in Greece.

Phelps did not dissapoint. In his first event, the 400-meter individual medley, he won with a world record time of 4:08.26 to take his first Olympic gold medal.

Though he lost out to Ian Thorpe in the 200m freestyle, the so-called "Race of the Century", the following days saw the young American scoop gold in the 200m butterfly, the 4x200 freestyle relay, the 100m butterfly and the 4x100m medley. Six gold and two bronze medals meant Phelps had achieved the second-best performance at the Olympics Games – he was second only to the legendary swimmer of 1972, Mark Spitz.

[...]

By the time London 2012 came round Phelps was, like Usain Bolt, a global star – a brand in his own right – and had even set up a foundation in his own name to promote healthy living and fitness for children. Having earlier announced his retirement, the world waited with bated breath to see if The Flying Fish could become the most decorated Olympian of all time.

[...]

It's not clear what the Michael Phelps way will be from this point on, but with 22 Games medals to his name, including an astonishing 18 golds, his record as the most decorated Olympian of all time seems likely to last for at least the rest of his retirement.

Adapted from <www.olympic.org/michael-phelps>. Accessed on July 03, 2015.

Language Reference

Regular Verbs		Irregular Verbs	
Base Form	Simple Past	Base Form	Simple Past
♦	♦	♦	♦
♦	♦	♦	♦
♦	♦	♦	♦
♦	♦	♦	♦
♦	♦	♦	♦
♦	♦	♦	♦
♦	♦	♦	♦
♦	♦	♦	♦
♦	♦	♦	♦
♦	♦	♦	♦

Unit 7

Modal Verbs

Modal Verbs (verbos modais) são auxiliares que conferem um significado específico aos verbos principais que os acompanham. *Modal verbs* são usados no presente ou no passado e posicionados antes dos verbos principais. Eles não precisam de outros verbos para as formas negativas e interrogativas e possuem a mesma forma para todas as pessoas do singular e do plural.

May

May geralmente é usado para expressar possibilidades, deduções ou pedir/conceder permissões (em situações de uso mais formais). A forma negativa do modal *may* é *may not*.

The principal **may not come** to our festival because she's on sick leave.

It **may rain** tonight. Look at the cloudy sky!

May I **have** your attention, Mr. Alves?

Can, Could

Can e *could* normalmente são usados para expressar habilidades, possibilidades, ou para pedir/conceder permissões (em situações mais informais). A forma negativa do modal *can* é *cannot* (*can't*). A forma negativa do modal *could* é *could not* (*couldn't*).

I **can't read** without my glasses. **Can** you **bring** them to me, honey?

Misfortunes **can happen** to anyone.

Can I **use** your calculator, Jarrod?

We **couldn't get** our driving licenses before we turned 18.

Finding a job **could be** good for you.

Teacher, **could** you **speak** slowly, please?

Should

Usamos o modal *should* para oferecer conselhos e fazer recomendações. A forma negativa de *should* é *should not* (*shouldn't*).

*Since I'm on a diet, I **shouldn't eat** sweets.*

*Thelma **should study** more for her final exams.*

***Should** we always **think** before talking?*

1. Read the ads below, identify the modal verbs and complete the sentence.

Extracted from <www.cdc.gov/media/dpk/2013/dpk-tips-campaign.html>.
Accessed on July 03, 2015.

Extracted from <theinspirationroom.com/daily/2012/al-ain-zoo-saving-water/>.
Accessed on July 03, 2015.

The modal verbs in the ads above express ♦ .

Language Reference

2. Choose the sentence that best explains the slogan of the campaign below.

Extracted from <moazedi.blogspot.com.br/2014/06/your-skin-color-shouldnt-dictate-your.html>. Accessed on July 03, 2015.

a. Your skin color can change who you are.
b. Your future could be different if you changed it.
c. Don't permit your skin color to command your future.

Unit 8

Present Continuous

O *Present Continuous* é normalmente usado para descrever ações que estão acontecendo no momento em que falamos. Para formar o *Present Continuous*, usamos o verbo *to be* no presente (*am*, *are* ou *is*) seguido do verbo principal acrescido da terminação -*ing*.

Para formar a forma negativa, usamos *not* depois do verbo *to be* e antes do verbo principal.

Na forma interrogativa, usamos o verbo *to be* antes do sujeito.

Observe os exemplos no quadro a seguir.

Affirmative	Negative	Interrogative
I **am** / I**'m reading** a magazine now.	I **am not** / I**'m not reading** a magazine now.	**Am** I **reading** a magazine now?
You **are** / You**'re talking** on the phone at the moment.	You **are not** / You **aren't talking** on the phone at the moment.	**Are** you **talking** on the phone at the moment?
He **is** / He**'s studying** French.	He **is not** / He **isn't studying** French.	**Is** he **studying** French?
She **is** / She**'s turning off** the lights.	She **is not** / She **isn't turning off** the lights.	**Is** she **turning off** the lights?

Affirmative	Negative	Interrogative
It **is** / It**'s snowing** heavily today.	It **is not** / It **isn't snowing** heavily today.	**Is** it **snowing** heavily today?
We **are** / We**'re eating** fast food.	We **are not** / We **aren't eating** fast food.	**Are** we **eating** fast food?
You **are** / You**'re working** on a new project.	You **are not** / You **aren't working** on a new project.	**Are** you **working** on a new project?
They **are** / They**'re playing** cards.	They **are not** / They **aren't playing** cards.	**Are** they **playing** cards?

Short Answers

| | Short Answers ||
	Affirmative	Negative
Is she listening to music?	Yes, she **is**.	No, she **isn't** (**is not**).
Are they recycling?	Yes, they **are**.	No, they **aren't** (**are not**).

É comum usarmos expressões de tempo como *now*, *at the moment* e *today* com o *Present Continuous*. Observe as frases abaixo.

*Cristina is doing the laundry **now**.*

*Are they writing their compositions **at the moment**?*

*It isn't raining **today**.*

Regras de ortografia para o acréscimo da terminação *-ing* no *Present Continuous*.

De maneira geral, acrescentamos a terminação *-ing* ao final dos verbos para formarmos o *Present Continuous*:

*go – go**ing***   *read – read**ing***

*ski – ski**ing***   *study – study**ing***

Porém, existem algumas exceções. Observe atentamente os casos abaixo.
- Verbos terminados em consoante + *-e*: eliminamos o *e* e acrescentamos *-ing*:

  *come – com**ing***   *use – us**ing***

- Verbos monossilábicos formados por consoante + vogal + consoante: dobramos a última consoante e acrescentamos a terminação *-ing*:

  *win – winn**ing***   *get – gett**ing***

- Verbos com duas ou mais sílabas, que tenham a última sílaba tônica: dobramos a última consoante e acrescentamos a terminação *-ing*:

  *permit – permitt**ing***   *begin – beginn**ing***

- Verbos terminados em *-ie*: substituímos *-ie* por *-y* e acrescentamos a terminação *-ing*:

  *tie – ty**ing***   *lie – ly**ing***

Language Reference

Language Reference

1. Choose the correct alternatives to complete the comic strips.

   a.

   - you could break up…
   - you're breaking up…

   b.

   - I'm not talking
   - I shouldn't talk

   c.

   - Can you imply
   - Are you implying

2. Complete the extract from the text *Technology and art: Engineering the future* using the verbs in parentheses in the Present Continuous tense.

Technology and art: Engineering the future

By Eyal Gever
Israeli 3D digital sculptor

[…]

All over the world, people ♦ (engineer) our future. The internet, digital fabrication, nanotech, biotech, self-modification, augmented reality, virtual reality, "the singularity" – you name it, all of this ♦ (alter) our lives and our view of the world and ourselves.

Scientists, software developers, inventors, entrepreneurs – but also musicians, visual artists, film-makers and designers – ♦ busy ♦ (create) new human experiences.

Thanks to them, not only is original art being made everywhere, but entirely new art forms ♦ (evolve) as well.

More and more artists ♦ (push) the boundaries of art, looking outside of what's perceived as "traditional" to incorporate other aspects into their work.

Art ♦ (become) less and less static, taking up many new different shapes, from printing digitally created sculptures in 3D to flash-mobs to photographers lining up hundreds of naked volunteers on the beach.

[…]

Extracted from <www.bbc.com/news/entertainment-arts-19576763>. Accessed on July 03, 2015.

Audio Scripts

Track 2, page 20, activities 2 and 3

What does it mean to be a global citizen?
To me, being a global citizen is understanding that everything is connected…
Making decisions based on the good of everyone, not just ourselves.
I am a global citizen.
Only one planet.
Loving people is the best way for you to be a global citizen.
If we know that we belong to the same humanity then we are brothers.
Everywhere is my country. I am a global citizen.
Depending on where a child is born, the access to basic human rights is so different.
We can't limit our concern to national values.
We live in a world that is inescapably connected. What we do in one place affects someone on the other side of the world.
I am interested in developing humanity no matter where they're found.
Ending extreme poverty.
I think that it is possible. Everything that has a beginning, has an end.
We have the energy to do it…We have the skills to do it.
What we do does really make a difference to other people.
I am a global citizen.
Each person must have something to contribute to make the world a better place.
That world has a lack of extreme poverty.
That world protects and sustains the environment.
That world is about equality.
That world is about access.
That world is about justice.
That world is about freedom.
That world is about health.
We should have a world by now where every child is born with the same rights to life.
That is the world we are fighting for…
Because the world we want and the world we're envisioning is the world we're gonna make and it's gonna be beautiful.
(0:00-1:44)

Transcribed from <teachunicef.org/explore/media/watch/global-citizenship>. Accessed on May 28, 2015.

Track 4, page 34, activities 2 and 3

Hi, my name is Justin Whittle, an undergraduate student studying Sustainable Agriculture and Food Security here at the University of Western Sydney.

Now, last year, I became increasingly aware of my future but also the challenges our generation will face. This is why myself and the UWS Office of Sustainability are planning to run a national conference to empower university students to discuss sustainable solutions and spread the message of hope.

This conference is completely different to anything before it, and we are giving undergraduate and honor students, like you, the chance to get your opinion, your idea, your solution to be heard by your peers and industry professionals. We want your solutions to help combat future challenges around food, the environment and ethics.

Each one poses complicated issues, but we want you to advocate game-changing ideas and out of the box solutions to empower our generation to make change and become leaders.

We want all university students from all over the world to come to UWS, Hawkesbury Campus, at Richmond, New South Wales, Australia, to champion innovative ideas for our sustainable future.

This is our world, our future, and we must be the drivers of change.

So, please come join me, here at Hawkesbury, and let's spread hope for a brighter future.
(0:00 - 1:55)

Transcribed from <www.youtube.com/watch?v=kQ8d5rhCMZw>. Accessed on June 5, 2015.

Track 6, pages 54 and 55, activities 2 and 3

Let's talk about Tidal. This is your music service.
Yeah.
You put together this unbelievable lineup of partners.
Yeah.
Some of the biggest names in all of music. And how is this different from the other music services?
I mean, it's better. It's better sound. It's better everything. No really…
The sound is a big thing, right.
I mean, they, they, they want, they want people to believe that you don't care about sound and quality. You know, they want you to believe that. Like, we don't care if it's hi-fi or not, but people will spend hours and, and months in studios mixing their sound and like, really crafting the sound. And they want, you know, people to hear and, you know, they pretend as if you don't care about it. But really, it's not even…forget, forget the sound because that's just a…a part of it. It's…If you think of streaming, it's the next thing. There was vinyl, then there was tape, then there was downloads and now we're streaming. That's just, that's just the na…I don't wanna keep swinging my hat…uhm, that's just the natural progress of, progress of what's

gonna happen and you just think of it like a big jukebox. You go in the jukebox. You know there's a barkeep. He curates it. He puts a couple of things in there. You put four dollars and you get five songs. But this way, you put nine dollars, you get 30 million songs. I mean...and you can take the jukebox and put it in your pocket and walk around. It's very simple.

It's a tiny little jukebox.

Yeah, a beautiful one.

And you got a big show going on tonight...

(0:00-1:17)

Transcribed from <www.youtube.com/watch?v=3O1IWXIF_TY>. Accessed on April 16, 2016.

Track 7, pages 68 and 69, activities 2 and 3

Hi! I'm Naomi, and I'm very excited to show you the world's greatest attractions.

This space-age modernist structure, designed by Oscar Niemeyer, houses the Niterói Contemporary Art Museum.

Situated at the bottom of a cliff, with a spectacular beach and view of surrounding small islands and distant mountains, this museum provides visitors with more than spectacular works of art.

The reflecting pool of blue-green ocean water beneath the structure was intended by Niemeyer to be the likeness of a flower.

The wall of windows surrounding the entirety of the building provides amazing natural light as well as an amazing view from any angle.

Finished in 1996, it has quickly become one of Brazil's national treasures.

From the intricate spiraling walkway to the view from the courtyard and beautiful art housed inside, this museum is a visual treat from start to finish.

Thank you for watching our Travel Video series.

See you next time!

(0:00-1:13)

Transcribed from <www.youtube.com/watch?v=WQnxUpuS13U>. Accessed on June 14, 2015.

Track 9, page 89, activities 2 and 3

So what would some of the healthiest breakfast foods be? I'm always surprised when I find out how many of my clients don't start their day off with a healthy breakfast. My theory on food is that, food is fuel and that we need to be fueling our bodies for the most active times of the day, which would be, you know, morning in the office, morning commuting, or whatever your morning activities would be. And when we skip breakfast we are starting on empty and we are putting unnecessary strain on the body. The other thing I believe about breakfast is that we don't necessarily have to have sweet sugary breakfast. We can have lunch for breakfast, we can have dinner for breakfast, we can have any food that we think is gonna fuel us for the kind of day we are gonna be having. And that's what I do with my clients as I work with them to balance out their meals so that they are using food to fuel them throughout the day. What would some typical breakfast foods be that I would suggest my clients incorporate into their diet? Oatmeal, berries, peanut butter, eggs, whole grain cereal or fruit salad, fruit smoothies, and whole grain toast. One of my favorite power breakfast, and I try to go for a power breakfast when I have a big morning or a big meeting that I have to make sure that I'm alert and have a lot of energy for would be whole grain bread with peanut butter. You are getting a high quality protein and you are getting complex carbohydrates and it will fuel you through your stressful busy day.

(0:00-1:47)

Transcribed from <www.howcast.com/videos/501746-healthiest-breakfast--foods-superfoods-guide/>. Accessed on June 15, 2015.

Track 11, page 102, activity 1

RENEE MONTAGNE, HOST:

This is Morning Edition, from NPR News. Good morning. I'm Renee Montagne.

STEVE INSKEEP, HOST:

And I'm Steve Inskeep. Today in "Your Health," counseling for young people. We're going to look at mental health on college campuses. But we begin with teens and exercise. It is well-known that routine physical activity benefits both body and mind. NPR's Patti Neighmond reports on a study that examines how much exercise can improve a teenager's attitude.

(0:00-0:24)

©2013 National Public Radio, Inc. Excerpt NPR news report titled "Why Exercise May Do A Teenage Mind Good" was originally broadcast on NPR's Morning Edition on January 7, 2013 and is used with the permission of NPR. Any unauthorized duplication is strictly prohibited.

Track 12, page 102, activity 2

PATTI NEIGHMOND, BYLINE: Researchers found physical activity can help teenagers in two powerful ways. One is confidence. Take 16-year-old volleyball player Jennifer Ramirez.

JENNIFER RAMIREZ: I've made something of myself, I feel. I feel like I'm not just like everyone else. Like, we all work hard to be something and like, it pays off and people recognize it. So it feels good.

NEIGHMOND: Then there's sociability – friends. Here's 17-year-old teammate Carly O'Sullivan.

CARLY O'SULLIVAN: I really don't care what other people think anymore. So, I can be myself around anyone. And I think a lot of people I've grown friendships with them because I really like myself.

Audio Scripts   185

Audio Scripts

NEIGHMOND: Both girls are on the Bogota High School volleyball team in northern New Jersey. And their experience gaining confidence and winning friends illustrates just what researchers in the Netherlands found when they surveyed 7,000 Dutch students between the ages of 11 and 16. The study appeared in the journal "Clinical Psychological Science." Yale University child psychologist Alan Kazdin is editor. He says the findings show just how bountiful the benefits of exercise can be.

ALAN KAZDIN: I think it'd be too strong to call it an elixir, but it has the broad effects of something like that.

NEIGHMOND: In the study, teenagers who took part in organized sports had a more positive self-image, and greater self-esteem than teens who weren't physically active. They were simply happier, says Kazdin, more grounded, and less likely to engage in problematic behavior.

[...]

(0:25-1:53)

©2013 National Public Radio, Inc. Excerpt NPR news report titled "Why Exercise May Do A Teenage Mind Good" was originally broadcast on NPR's Morning Edition on January 7, 2013 and is used with the permission of NPR. Any unauthorized duplication is strictly prohibited.

Track 14, page 122, activity 2

Society
Originally by Jerry Hannan

It's a mystery to me
We have a greed with which we have agreed
And you think you have to want more than you need
Until you have it all, you won't be free

Society, you're a crazy breed
I hope you're not lonely without me

When you want more than you have, you think you need
And when you think more than you want, your thoughts begin to bleed
I think I need to find a bigger place
Cause when you have more than you think, you need more space

Society, you're a crazy breed
I hope you're not lonely without me
Society, crazy indeed
Hope you're not lonely without me

There's those thinking more or less, less is more
But if less is more, how you keepin score?
Means for every point you make your level drops
Kinda like you're startin' from the top
And you can't do that

Society, you're a crazy breed
I hope you're not lonely without me
Society, crazy indeed
I hope you're not lonely without me
Society, have mercy on me
I hope you're not angry if I disagree
Society, you're crazy indeed
I hope you're not lonely without me

Extracted from <www.azlyrics.com/lyrics/eddievedder/society.html>.
Accessed on September 5, 2015.

Track 15, page 136, activity 2

Hey, it's Dallas Travers the actress advocate with another edition of Acting Business Bytes.

Let's talk about e-mail. Have you ever had the experience, I know I have, of opening an e-mail from a friend or a colleague, and there is so much written in that e-mail that immediately you think to yourself I don't have the time for this. I'll get to this e-mail later, and that e-mail ends up sitting in your inbox for a really long time because it feels like a lot of work.

I get those a lot. It's actually really surprising to me how often I will receive an e-mail from an actor or a student that is so long in explanation that it never really gets to the point. And I tell you, those e-mails are frustrating to a degree, because it's hard for me to help you when you are not being clear. So the principle of simplicity and being concise is so important when it comes to your professional e-mails, and what I would like to do is share a few tips to help you be perceived as a professional, but also to help you get the feedback you want from the e-mails that you are sending. Often times, if you don't hear back from someone, it's probably because the e-mail you sent created too much work for them. So I'll give you a couple of tips. Then I'm actually going to give you a formula to follow when it comes to sending e-mails. [...]

(0:00-1:24)

Transcribed from <www.youtube.com/watch?v=jBIG3_YVub0>. Accessed on June 24, 2015.

Track 16, page 137, activity 3

[...] So the principle of simplicity and being concise is so important when it comes to your professional e-mails, and what I would like to do is share a few tips to help you be perceived as a professional, but also to help you get the feedback you want from the e-mails that you are sending. Often times, if you don't hear back from someone, it's probably because the e-mail you sent created too much work for them. So I'll give you a couple of tips. Then I'm actually going to give you a formula to follow when it comes to sending e-mails. [...]

(0:53-1:24)

Transcribed from <www.youtube.com/watch?v=jBIG3_YVub0>. Accessed on June 24, 2015.

EXTRA RESOURCES

Unit 1

Go to the following site and get to know better about global citizenship.
<www. globalcitizen.org/en/>. Accessed on May 30, 2015.

WATSON, Susan. *Global Citizenship*. Australia: Macmillan Education, 2009.
The book helps students understand what global citizenship is and what they can do to improve global environment as well as people's well-being.

JACKSON, Michael. *"Heal The World"*. Lyrics by: Michael Jackson, Dangerous Album, 1991.
The lyrics are about creating a better world for future generations. Available at <www.azlyrics.com/lyrics/michaeljackson/healtheworld.html>. Accessed on September 5, 2015.

Unit 2

ALLEN ,Vinit. *The Sustainable World Sourcebook*. 4th edition. EUA: Sustainable World Coalition, 2014.
This book gives readers a better idea of the major global issues we face nowadays, as well as the most promising solutions.

Go to the site of Western Sydney University and get to know better about the 2015 Sustainability Conference.
<www.uws.edu.au/s4s/students_for_sustainability_conference/about_s4>. Accessed on November 3, 2015.

Read about sustainability and sustainable development at
<www.un.org/en/sustainablefuture/sustainability.shtml> and
<www.sd-commission.org.uk/pages/what-is-sustainable-development.html>. Accessed on June 05, 2015.

HOME – Nosso planeta, nossa casa. Direction: Yann Arthus-Bertrand. 2009. Duration: 93 minutes.
The movie shows the catastrophic situation of the Earth and alerts people to change the way they live. Available at <www.youtube.com/watch?v=jqxENMKaeCU">. Accessed on June 5, 2015.

Unit 3

Read about Tidal, the most recent streaming music service at
<www.techtudo.com.br/noticias/noticia/2015/04/tidal-lossless-saiba-o-que-o-novo-rival-do-spotify-tem-de-tao-especial.html>. Accessed on June 08, 2015.

August Rush: O Som do Coração. Warner Bros Pictures. 2007. Duration: 114 minutes.
The movie tells the story of an orphaned musical prodigy who uses his gift to find his birth parents.

Unit 4

Get to know more about MoMa, the Museum of Modern Art, at
<www.moma.org>. Accessed on June 14, 2015.

Read about CowParade, the world's largest public art event at
<www.cowparade.com>. Accessed on June 14, 2015.

Read about MAC de Niterói (Museu de Arte Moderna de Niterói) at
<www.macniteroi.com.br>. Accessed on June 17, 2015.

Watch a video about the interactive museum *Art in Island* in Manila, the Philippines, where visitors interact with the art, at
<www.youtube.com/watch?v=94eV2k1nikc>. Accessed on June 14, 2015.

EXTRA RESOURCES

Unit 5

MCKEITH. Gillian. *Você é o que você come!*: o poder da alimentação natural. São Paulo: Alegro, 2004.

The author of the book has become well-known because she helped English people change their unhealthy eating habits. The book shows everyone is able to change habits.

What Brazil's dietary guidelines can teach us about healthy eating.

This Australian news article compares Brazil's dietary guidelines to theirs and declares that they can learn a lot from us. Available at <www.smh.com.au/lifestyle/diet-and-fitness/what-brazils-dietary-guidelines-can-teach-us-about-healthy-eating-20150416-1mmhd6.html>. Accessed on November 5, 2015.

The War on Wheat. 2015. Duration: 38 minutes.

The documentary reveals the minimal influence science has had in dissuading people from the belief that genetically modified crops present a serious health threat.

Unit 6

LEWIS, Michael. *The Blind Side: Evolution of a Game.* USA: W.W. Norton & Company, 2006.

The story of Michael Oher, a homeless child whose mother is addicted to crack. He doesn't know his father, and he doesn't know how to read or write. He has his life transformed when he is adopted by a rich family and he discovers family love and his love for football.

Take a sports quiz of the week and have fun at <www.theguardian.com/sport/2015/jun/19/sports-quiz-week-euro-u21s-us-open-copaamerica-nba-finals>. Accessed on June 20, 2015.

Watch a video in which parents and teenagers discuss the importance of a healthy lifestyle, family sports, and the types of daily activity that keep them active, at

<raisingchildren.net.au/articles/fitness_health_teenagers_video.html/context/1194>. Accessed on June 20, 2015.

Unit 7

Read an article about the consumers' lifestyles in Brazil at

<www.euromonitor.com/consumer-lifestyles-in-brazil/report>. Accessed on June 21, 2015.

This article presents some interesting facts about the use of the Internet in Brazil.
<www.forbes.com/sites/ricardogeromel/2013/10/28/internet-in-brazil-key-hard-facts-you-must-know/>. Accessed on November 11, 2015.

Wall Street: Money Never Sleeps. Direction: Oliver Stone. Twentieth Century Fox Film Corporation. 2010. Duration: 133 minutes.

The movie tells the story of a young and impatient stockbroker who does anything to get to the top.

Unit 8

Read about the offline digital library that has been created by a non-profit organization and is available for students at Ahmadu Bello University in Nigeria at

<learningenglish.voanews.com/content/bringing-internet-closer-helps-students/2842454.html>. Accessed on September 5, 2015.

Irregular Verbs List

Base Form	Past	Past Participle	Translation
be	was, were	been	ser, estar
become	became	become	tornar-se
begin	began	begun	começar
break	broke	broken	quebrar
bring	brought	brought	trazer
build	built	built	construir
buy	bought	bought	comprar
catch	caught	caught	pegar
choose	chose	chosen	escolher
come	came	come	vir
cost	cost	cost	custar
deal	dealt	dealt	lidar
do	did	done	fazer
draw	drew	drawn	desenhar
drink	drank	drunk	beber
drive	drove	driven	dirigir
eat	ate	eaten	comer
feel	felt	felt	sentir
fight	fought	fought	lutar
find	found	found	achar
forget	forgot	forgotten	esquecer
forsake	forsook	forsaken	abandonar; desistir de
get	got	got(ten)	conseguir
give	gave	given	dar
go	went	gone	ir
grow	grew	grown	crescer; cultivar
have	had	had	ter
hear	heard	heard	ouvir
know	knew	known	saber

Base Form	Past	Past Participle	Translation
leave	left	left	deixar, partir
make	made	made	fazer
mean	meant	meant	significar
meet	met	met	encontrar
overcome	overcame	overcome	superar
pay	paid	paid	pagar
proofread	proofread	proofread	revisar
put	put	put	colocar
read	read	read	ler
rise	rose	risen	subir; erguer-se
say	said	said	dizer
see	saw	seen	ver
seek	sought	sought	procurar
sell	sold	sold	vender
send	sent	sent	enviar
set	set	set	ajustar; marcar
show	showed	showed/shown	mostrar
shrink	shrank	shrunk	encolher
sing	sang	sung	cantar
sit	sat	sat	sentar
speak	spoke	spoken	falar
swim	swam	swum	nadar
take	took	taken	levar
teach	taught	taught	ensinar
tell	told	told	dizer
think	thought	thought	pensar
understand	understood	understood	entender
wear	wore	worn	vestir, usar
win	won	won	vencer, ganhar
write	wrote	written	escrever

Glossary

ability: habilidade
access: acesso
accident: acidente
achievement: conquista, realização, resultado
act: agir, atuar
actor: ator
actually: na verdade
ad campaign: anúncio publicitário
added: acrescentado(a)
advance: avançar
advocate: advogado(a)
affordable: acessível
agree: concordar
aim: objetivo, propósito
amazing: surpreendente
anchor: ancorar
angle: ângulo
appealing: atraente, atrativo(a)
approach: enfoque, método
art: arte
artist: artista
aspire: almejar
athlete: atleta
attend: participar
audience: público
augment: melhorar
available: disponível
aware: ciente
awareness: conscientização
back up: fazer cópia reserva de um arquivo ou programa
beginning: começo, início
benefit: benefício
blind: deficiente visual
blinking: piscante
bolt down: comer rapidamente

boot up: fazer a inicialização
breed: espécie
brochure: folheto
call for participants/participation: convocação
career: carreira
catchy: atraente, cativante
challenge: desafiar; desafio
change: alterar, mudar
charity: caridade
chromatic: cromático(a)
citizen: cidadão
citizenship: cidadania
collect: colecionar, colher (informações)
college: universidade
come up with: encontrar; inventar
comic strip: tirinha
community: comunidade
concerned: interessado(a), preocupado(a)
concise: conciso(a)
confirm: confirmar
consumption: consumo
consumerism: consumismo
contain: conter
contribute: contribuir
convey: expressar, transmitir
conveyed: expressado(a), transmitido(a)
costume: fantasia, traje
count on: contar com
create: criar
credential: qualificação
customer: consumidor(a)
customize: personalizar
cut down: reduzir

daily: diário(a)
decrease: diminuir, reduzir
defend: defender
develop: desenvolver
deviate: divergir
device: dispositivo
dietitian: dietista
disability: deficiência, incapacidade
disagree: discordar
displayed: apresentado(a), exibido(a), mostrado(a)
diversity: diversidade
draft: rascunho
draw attention: chamar atenção
drinking water: água potável
eco-friendly: ecológico(a)
employer: empregador(a)
empower: delegar poderes a
encourage: encorajar, incentivar
engage: dedicar-se, engajar-se
environment: meio ambiente
equality: igualdade
ethnicity: etnia
excitement: entusiasmo
exhibition: exposição
expect: esperar (ter expectativa de)
exposition: exposição
extract: trecho
fat: gordura
feature: apresentar; característica
fee: tarifa, taxa
fencing: esgrima
figure out: compreender
find out: adivinhar, descobrir
follow: seguir
former: anterior, ex
free: gratuito(a)

freedom: liberdade
gain weight: engordar
genre: gênero
give up: desistir
go down: cair o sinal da internet
great: excelente
greed: cobiça, ganância
harm: prejudicar
health: saúde
healthy: saudável
humanity: humanidade
illegally: irregularmente, ilegalmente
impaired: debilitado(a)
impairment: deficiência
improve: melhorar
in time: com antecedência
increase: ampliar, aumentar
industry: indústria
inequality: desigualdade
infer: inferir
influence: influência
injustice: injustiça
intend: pretender
interdependence: interdependência
introduce: apresentar-se
invitation: convite
invite: convidar
issue: assunto, questão
junk food: comida sem qualidade
killing: destruição
kinetic: cinético, dinâmico
knowledge: conhecimento
lack of: falta de
landfill: aterro
leak: perder (memória de computador)
learn: aprender

Glossary

legend: lenda
library: biblioteca
light: luz
living being: ser vivo
log off: terminar a sessão
longevity: longevidade
lower: baixar, diminuir, reduzir; mais baixa, reduzida
lunch: almoço
magazine: revista
magnificent: deslumbrante, magnífico(a)
main: principal
major in: formar-se
make sense: fazer sentido
manage: administrar, lidar com
manufacturer: fabricante
market analyst: analista de mercado
meal: refeição
meaning: significado
meaningful: significativo(a)
meditate: meditar
motherland: pátria
museum: museu
music: música
neighbor (US) / **neighbour** (UK): vizinho
neighborhood (US) / **neighbourhood** (UK): bairro
nutrition coach: nutricionista
nutritionist: nutricionista
opening: abertura, lançamento
overheat: superaquecer
overview: visão geral
overweight: obeso(a)
owner: proprietário(a)
painting: pintura, quadro, tela

paralympic: paralímpico
parent: pai ou mãe
parking: estacionamento
participate: participar
peer: colega
persuasive: convincente
piece of advice: conselho
piracy: pirataria
planet: planeta
political: político(a)
pollution: poluição
pool: piscina
pop up: aparecer, surgir
power: energia, força, poder
preference: preferência
pretend: fingir
price: preço
priceless: incalculável, inestimável; precioso
print out: imprimir
profile: perfil
promote: promover
publish: publicar
push: empurrar
raw: cru
reach: alcançar, atingir
reality: realidade
realize (someone's dream): realizar um sonho
recommendation: recomendação
reflecting: que reflete
register: cadastrar, inscrever, matricular
rehearsal: ensaio
rehearse: ensaiar
reliable: confiável
research: pesquisar; pesquisa
resource: recurso

role: função, papel
run out of: ficar sem
scarcity: escassez
schedule: agendar
sculptor: escultor(a)
seafood: frutos do mar
self-taught: autodidata
sensitize: sensibilizar
set up: instalar
share: compartilhar, dividir
shooter: atirador(a)
shooting: tiro
shortage: escassez
shrink: encolher
sight: visão
skill: competência, habilidade
smash: golpear
snack: aperitivo, lanche
social worker: assistente social
society: sociedade
solution: resolução, solução
song: canção, música
spectacular: espetacular
stay: ficar
store: armazenar
stream: transmitir ou receber continuamente dados pela internet
submit: apresentar, submeter
summit: conferência
survey: pesquisa
sustainability: sustentabilidade
sustainable: sustentável
take action: agir, tomar uma atitude
take note: tomar nota de
take part: participar
take turns: revezar
technology: tecnologia

techy: tecnológico(a)
tempting: tentador(a)
theater acting: atuação em um teatro
tone: tom
tool: ferramenta
training/training course: treinamento
trash: lixo
troubleshooting: resolução de problemas
turn on: ligar
turn to: concentrar; dirigir
tweak: ajustar, refinar
undergraduate student: aluno(a) de graduação
urge: encorajar, estimular
useful: útil
value: valorizar; valor
variety: variedade
viewer: espectador(a)
viewing: visitação
water consumption: consumo de água
whatever: qualquer
wheelchair: cadeira de roda
while: enquanto
work out: exercitar-se
world: mundo
worldwide: mundial, universal

Bibliography

ABREU-TARDELLI, L. S.; CRISTOVÃO, V. L. L. (Org.). *Linguagem e educação*: o ensino e aprendizagem de gêneros textuais. Campinas: Mercado de Letras, 2009.

BEZERRA, M. A.; DIONISIO, A. P.; MACHADO, A. R. (Org.). *Gêneros textuais & ensino*. São Paulo: Parábola Editorial, 2010.

BRASIL/SEMTEC. *PCN+ Ensino Médio: Orientações educacionais complementares aos Parâmetros Curriculares Nacionais*. Volume 1: Linguagens, códigos e suas tecnologias. Brasília, DF: MEC/SEMTEC, 2002. Disponível em: <portal.mec.gov.br/seb/arquivos/pdf/02Linguagens.pdf>. Acesso em: 12 julho 2015.

BRASIL/SEMTEC. *Linguagens, Códigos e suas Tecnologias*: Orientações Curriculares para o Ensino Médio. Capítulo 3. Conhecimentos de línguas estrangeiras. 2006. Disponível em <http://portal.mec.gov.br/seb/arquivos/pdf/book_volume_01_internet.pdf>. Acesso em 12 julho 2015.

COPE, B. & KALANTZIS, M. Multiliteracies: The Beginning of an Idea. In: COPE, B. & KALANTZIS, M. (Eds.). *Multiliteracies: Literacy Learning and The Design of Social Futures*. London: Routledge, 2000. p. 3-8.

CROSS, D. *Large Classes in Action*. Hertfordshire: Prentice Hall International, 1995.

DIONISIO, A. P. et al. (org.) *Gêneros textuais & ensino*. Rio de Janeiro: Lucerna, 2002, p. 19-36.

Diretrizes Curriculares Nacionais da Educação Básica. Ministério da Educação, 2013.

FREIRE, Paulo. *Pedagogia da autonomia*: saberes necessários à prática educativa. São Paulo: Paz e Terra, 1996.

GRELLET, F. *Developing Reading Skills*. Cambridge: Cambridge University Press, 1981.

HEIDE, Ann & STILBORNE, Linda. *Guia do professor para a internet*: completo e fácil. Trad. Edson Furmankiewz. 2. ed. Porto Alegre: Artmed, 2000.

HOFFMANN, Jussara. *Avaliar para promover*: as setas do caminho. Porto Alegre: Mediação, 2001.

LAPKOSKI, G. A. O. *Do texto ao sentido*: teoria e prática de leitura em língua inglesa. Curitiba: Ibpex, 2011.

MARCUSCHI, L. A. "Gêneros textuais: definição e funcionalidade". In: DIONISIO, A. P. et al. (org.) *Gêneros textuais & ensino*. Rio de Janeiro: Lucerna, 2002, p. 19-36.

MARTINEZ, P. *Didática de línguas estrangeiras*. São Paulo: Parábola Editorial, 2009.

MOITA-LOPES, L. P. "Ensino de inglês como espaço de embates culturais e de políticas da diferença." In: GIMENEZ, T. et al. (Org.). *Perspectivas educacionais e o ensino de inglês na escola pública*. Pelotas: Educat, 2005.

_____. *Oficina de linguística aplicada*. Campinas: Mercado de Letras, 2000.

RAIMES, A. *Techniques in Teaching Writing*. New York: Oxford University Press, 1983.

RICHARDS, J. C.; RENANDYA, W. A. (Ed.). *Methodology in Language Teaching*: an anthology of current practice. New York: Cambridge University Press, 2002.

RODRIGUES, D. (Org.). *Inclusão e educação*: doze olhares sobre a educação inclusiva. São Paulo: Summus, 2006.

ROJO, Roxane; MOURA, Eduardo. *Multiletramentos na escola*. São Paulo: Parábola Editorial, 2012.

SCHNEUWLY, Bernard & DOLZ, Joaquim. *Gêneros orais e escritos na escola*. Campinas: Mercado das Letras, 2004.

SOUZA, Adriana Grade Fiori et al. *Leitura em língua inglesa*: uma abordagem instrumental. São Paulo: Disal, 2005.

TOMLINSON, B. *Developing Materials for Language Teaching*. Londres: Continuum, 2003.

VYGOTSKY, L. S. *Pensamento e linguagem*. São Paulo: Martins Fontes, 1993.

WALESKO, A. M. H. *Compreensão oral em língua inglesa*. Curitiba: Ibpex, 2010.